Pilgrims' Guide to America

✠ U.S. Catholic Shrines and Centers of Devotion

Our Sunday Visitor Publishing Division
Our Sunday Visitor, Inc.
Huntington, Indiana 46750

D1366273

ISBN: 0-87973-469-8
LCCCN: 91-66664

PRINTED IN THE UNITED STATES OF AMERICA

Cover design by Monica Watts
Editorial production by Kelley L. Renz
469

TABLE OF CONTENTS

SHRINES BY STATE

INTRODUCTION

A Catholic Shrine is a holy place dedicated to God, one of the Persons of the Trinity, the Blessed Virgin, or one or more of the saints. Devotions are held on a regular basis and attract persons from outside the parish or the immediate vicinity. Attention usually focuses on a relic, significant statue, icon or painting. Sometimes the holy place is the site of an apparition or an important and/or miraculous event.

Shrines are normally located in churches but can be found in other places as well: monasteries, seminaries, motherhouses of religious orders and college campuses. Such devotional sanctuaries can even be found in prisons, hospitals, insane asylums and cemeteries.

Shrines are by no means a uniquely Catholic or Christian phenomena. From time immemorial people have considered certain places sacred. To the primitive, deity is not ubiquitous but localized. When people lived a momadic existence, certain mountains, groves, caverns and other natural sites were considered holy. But with the coming of agriculture, indoor sanctuaries such as temples and churches came into prominence.

Shrines and pilgrimages are found in many non-Christian religions; they are integral to Hinduism, Islam and Shinto, among others. And they are part of our Old Testament heritage. Each year all Jews were required to come to Jerusalem for the three traditional pilgrimage festivals: Passover, the Feasts of Weeks (Pentecost) and Tabernacles (Booths). Jesus observed these practices while on earth. (The Last Supper was a Passover meal.)

After Christ's death, pilgrims began to frequent the locations of significant events in his life. Records indicate that pilgrimages were made to Palestine and Jerusalem as early as the second century. With the legalization of Christianity by Constantine in the fourth century, pious travelers flocked to the Holy Land. Perhaps the most famous of these was the Empress Helena who was responsible for discovering the location of so many relics of the life and death of the Son of Man, including the true cross.

Nor was Palestine the only destination for the early Christian traveler. The tombs of St. Peter in Rome and of St. James in Compostella, Spain attracted many pilgrims, as did the burial sites of the many Christian martyrs. The Roman liturgical calendar of A.D. 354 noted twenty-nine local shrines frequented annually by the faithful.

As the new faith spread throughout the Middle East, Europe and North Africa, the number of saints and martyrs increased considerably. During the Middle Ages pilgrims swarmed the shrines of these Christian heroes.

With the fall of the Holy Land to Islam, a new type of pilgrim appeared: the Crusader. These Christian warriors attempted to wrest control of Palestine from the Muslims.

Ultimately they failed, but their efforts gained access to the holy places for future generations. During the Middle Ages one factor that greatly increased the visitation of the shrines of the saints was the requirement by confessors of a penitential pilgrimage, in place of humiliating and lengthy public penances. Another medieval custom was that of granting indulgences to those who visited certain holy sanctuaries. This practice reached its high point during the Holy Year of 1300 when 200,000 pilgrims descended on Rome.

Among the more important medieval shrines were those of St. Martin (Tours), St. Thomas a Becket (Canterbury), St. Boniface (Fulda) and St. Francis (Assisi). The more popular Marian sanctuaries included those at Walsingham, Chartes and Loreto.

With the coming of the Renaissance and Reformation, the practice of visiting shrines came under attack. The Augsburg Confession denounced pilgrimages as "childish and useless works." Many shrines were destroyed or put to other uses by the Protestant reformers and in much of Northern Europe the pilgrim tradition died.

Yet this was not the end. Catholic Southern and Eastern Europe remained faithful. In the lands of the Counter-Reformation, the old pilgrimage places retained their attraction, while new ones came into existence. Meanwhile, the Catholic faith had spread far beyond the boundaries of Europe. Shrines made their appearance as far away as India, China and the Americas. Among the more popular sanctuaries in the New World were those at St. Anne de Beaupre (Canada), Cobre (Cuba), Guadalupe (Mexico), Lujan (Argentine) and Aparecida (Brazil.)

In this country, the first shrine established was the one dedicated to Our Lady of La Leche at St. Augustine, Florida. Other Spanish pilgrimage centers came into existence in Texas, New Mexico and California. Next came the French with their dedication to St. Anne, Our Lady of Prompt Succor and St. Roch. Each succeeding wave of immigrants brought with them the devotions popular in their native land: we now have shrines in honor of Our Lady of Czestochowa, St. Patrick and *Nuestra Senora de San Juan de los Lagos*. In addition to these, there are sanctuaries honoring saints popularized by certain religious orders. (For example, Redemptionists promote Our Lady of Perpetual Help and the Franciscans encourage devotion to St. Anthony of Padua.) Then there are shrines honoring American saints like Mother Cabrini and St. John Neumann. And, of course, there are the ever popular Lourdes grottos and pilgrimage places honoring St. Jude, St. Joseph and Our Lady of Fatima. Altogether there are more than 360 shrines and other centers of devotion.

At this point it is necessary to clarify a term: a center of devotion is a place where a particular saint or Person of the Trinity is the object of much popular veneration. However, it is not generally referred to as a shrine nor is it well known enough to draw many pilgrims from outside the parish or the immediate vicinity. It might be thought of as a potential—as opposed to an actual—shrine.

I have purposely excluded from this book places whose claim to fame is their antiquity or their cultural, artistic or historic value. Nor have I included shrines in convents, schools, seminaries and monasteries which are not frequented by those not connected with the institution. I have tried to include as many shrines and centers of devotion as possible, but no doubt there are others that have not come to my attention. All such omissions are regretted.

Lastly, I would like to thank the many pastors, shrine directors, archivists and others without whose help I would not have been able to write this book.

Go with God.
Yours in Christ and Mary,
J. Anthony Moran
March 19
St. Joseph Day

Note: Readers are urged to contact the shrines/centers of devotion before traveling as times of visitation may change. If no direct address is given in a specific listing, the shrine/center of devotion is easily located. No visitation times are given for outdoor shrines.

PART ONE:
SHRINES OF THE EAST

Connecticut
Maine
Massachusetts
New Hampshire
New Jersey
New York
Pennsylvania
Rhode Island
Vermont

CONNECTICUT

BRIDGEPORT

1. Shrine of St. Margaret's, 2539 North Park Avenue

The picturesque sanctuary has a series of grottos, shrines and chapels honoring Our Lord, the Blessed Virgin and the saints. The wooded area with its statues, gardens and waterfalls provides a place for quiet meditation.
(Daylight hours)

LITCHFIELD

2. Lourdes in Litchfield, Route 118

Begun in 1956, The Montfort Missionaries' shrine was completed two years later during the centenary of the apparition of the Blessed Virgin to St. Bernadette at Lourdes. Built using local field stone, the grotto is modeled after the original in France. Winding for a quarter of a mile up a wooded hill to the Crucifixion scene, the Way of the Cross is one of the principal attractions here. (The stations are life-like bronze figures.) Also of interest are shrines dedicated to the Sacred Heart of Jesus, St. Michael, St. Jude and St. Louis de Montfort. The shrine is open to pilgrims all year round.

NEW HAVEN

3. Shrine of the Infant of Prague; St. Mary's Church, 5 Hillhouse Avenue

Veneration of the "Little King" has its origin in 17th century Czechoslovakia. From the Carmelite Church of Our Lady of Victory in Prague, devotion has spread throughout the Catholic world. The New Haven Dominican shrine founded in 1946 by Fr. Vincent R. Burnell has for its focal point the right side altar dedicated to the Infant Savior. There are four Solemn Novenas a year. Persons unable to attend may send their petitions by mail.
(7:00 a.m. to 6:00 p.m.)

MAINE

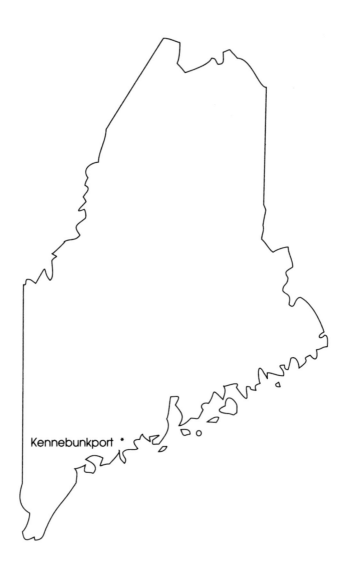

Kennebunkport *

KENNEBUNKPORT

4. St. Anthony Monastery and Shrines

In 1947, Lithuanian Franciscans purchased the William A. Rogers estate on the Kennebunk River and transformed it into a friary and shrine. Famous for its Lourdes Grotto, St. Anthony Shrine and the Chapel of the Stations of the Cross, the monastery grounds also boasts the Vatican Pavilion Monument, the Lithuanian Wayside Cross and the Infant of Prague Chapel. Overnight accommodations are available during the summer pilgrimage season.
(Daylight hours)

MASSACHUSETTS

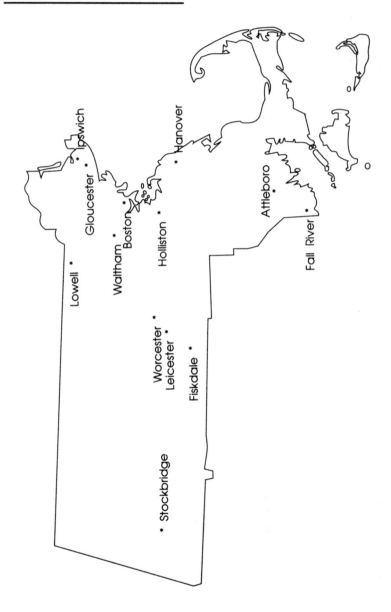

ATTLEBORO

5. Shrine of Our Lady of La Salette, Route 118

To commemorate the Nineteenth century apparition of the Blessed Virgin to two shepherd children in the French Alps, the La Salette Fathers established this shrine in 1953. Located midway between Boston and Providence, the Marian sanctuary is one of the most popular in the country. Famous for its Christmas time Festival of Lights, ethnic pilgrimages, and the summer Festival of Flowers, the 17-acre shrine is open all year. Among its attractions are the Garden of the Apparition of Our Lady of La Salette, the Rosary Garden and the Way of the Cross with its Calvery and Holy Stairs. In addition, there are Our Lady's Rose Garden and shrines honoring St. Joseph and St. Francis. A cafeteria, gift shop and book store are also available.

Mailing address: 947 Park Street, Attleboro, MA
(9:00 a.m. to 9:00 p.m.)

BOSTON

6. Saint Anthony Shrine, 100 Arch Street

Located in the heart of downtown Boston, the Workers' Chapel, as it is called, serves shoppers and those employed in the area. Dedicated in 1955, this shrine is situated on the lower floors of a 10-story Franciscan monastary whose facade is graced by an 18-foot crucifix. There are two main churches, one at street level and the other on the second floor.
(6:00 a.m. to 7:00 p.m.)

7. St. Clement's Archdiocesan Eucharistic Shrine, 1105 Boylston Street

This stone Gothic structure with detached towers was once the Universalist Church of the Redemption. Purchased by the Archdiocese of Boston and dedicated in 1928, St. Clement's serves as an official center for adoration of the Blessed Sacrament. Open everyday from 7:00 a.m. to 7:00 p.m., the shrine is administered by the Oblates of the Virgin Mary.
(Always open)

8. Lourdes Center, 698 Beacon Street

Founded in 1950 by Cardinal Cushing of Boston, with the cooperation of Bishop Theas of Tarbes-Lourdes, France, the Center exists to promote devotion to Our Lady of Lourdes in America. At first headquartered in the basement of Our Lady of Victories' Rectory, the Marist Fathers moved to Beacon Street thirteen years later. The Center distributes Lourdes water, organizes pilgrimages to the site of the apparitions to St. Bernadette, and serves as source of information on the French shrine. Novenas to the Immaculata are held in the Center's Chapel of Our Lady of Lourdes each Thursday. *(8:00 a.m. to 4:30 p.m. M-F; 11:00 a.m. to 4:30 p.m. Sat.; Closed Sun.)*

9. Basilica of Our Lady of Perpetual Help, Mission Church, 1545 Tremont Street

The original icon-style painting of Our Lady of Perpetual Help was produced in the 13th or 14th century. Though the wonder-working portrait was in the hands of the Augustinians for several centuries, in 1866 it was transferred to the new Redemptorist church of St. Alphonsus Ligouri in Rome. The following year it received a papal crown. Copies of the painting were made, touched to original, then sent to Redemptorist houses in the United States. One such was enthroned above the main altar at Mission Church in 1871. When a new much larger church was built seven years later, a chapel in honor of Our Lady of Perpetual Help was constructed in the transept on the left side. Here occurred a series of dramatic cures which brought national attention in 1883. Mission Church is now the foremost shrine to the Redemptorist Madonna in the United States. Elevated to the rank of a basilica in 1954, the most prominent features of the Romanesque structure are its twin towers on the facade and the great dome. Above the main altar stands an impressive statue of Our Mother of Sorrows and to the right is a chapel which enshrines the body of St. Nazarius the Martyr brought here from Rome in 1873. Novenas to Our Lady of Perpetual Help are held every Wednesday.
(6:30 a.m. to 7:30 p.m., enter through rectory)

10. Our Lady of Fatima Shrine, St. Gabriel's Church, 139 Washington Street (Brighton)

The Marian sanctuary owes its existence to a group of dedicated Boston area laymen called the Crusaders of Fatima. Built in 1968, the shrine is octagonal in shape, with glass panels enclosing it on five sides. Located on the grounds of St. Gabriel Church, the shrine has a relic consisting of a piece of the top branch of the holm oak tree above which Our Lady appeared at Fatima.
(1:30 p.m. to 4:30 p.m. M-F; 9:00 a.m. to 6:00 p.m. Sat. and Sun.)

11. The Madonna, Queen of the Universe National Shrine, 11 Orient Avenue (East Boston)

Located on the grounds of the Don Orione Home for the Elderly operated by the Sons of Divine Providence, the shrine's focal point is a 32-foot statue of the Madonna, said to be the tallest in the country. The image, designed by Arrigo Minerbi, is an exact copy of the one that stands at the summit of Monte Mario in Rome. Though begun in 1956, there have been long pauses in the construction of the Madonna National Shrine. The main church of the shrine was dedicated by Cardinal Bernard Law of Boston in 1987, during the Marian Year. A high point in the sanctuary's history came in 1960 when the Boston Archdiocese's official reception for Cardinal Montini of Milan, soon to become Pope Paul VI, was held there.
(8:00 a.m. to 8:00 p.m.)

FALL RIVER

12. St. Anne's Church and Shrine, 818 Middle Street

As Fr. Adrien de Montaubricq was about to bless the church's cornerstone, the platform on which he was standing collapsed. When he realized the extent of his injuries, he promised St. Anne that if he recovered he would name the house of worship in her honor. (He had intended to dedicate it to St. Clothilda). As might have been expected, the priest regained his health. There has been a July 18-26 Solemn Novena to the mother of the Blessed Virgin here since 1872, but the first organized pilgrimages did not occur until twenty years later. The present shrine church was dedicated in 1906. The Roman-Byzantine structure has two levels. The upper church is of blue Vermont marble. To the left of the main altar is a statue of St. Anne modeled after the one in Beaupre, Canada. But it is the shrine to the grandmother of Jesus in the lower church which attracts the attention of pilgrims. Since 1928, there has been a Perpetual Novena to Good St. Anne. The parish is administered by the Dominicans. *(7:00 a.m. to 7:00 p.m.)*

FISKDALE

13. St. Anne's Shrine, 16 Church Street

In 1879, when his health was failing, Msgr. Elzear Brochu promised the grandmother of Jesus that if he recovered he would build a shrine in her honor. His prayers were answered and four years later St. Anne's Church was built. On the Sunday following the Feast of the Mother of the Blessed Virgin, 1888, Mrs. Jean-Baptiste Houde was cured of Dropsy as she approached the altar to receive Communion. Five years later, an authenticated relic of the saint was obtained from the Shrine of St. Anne de Beaupre in Canada. As crowds increased, an outdoor chapel was constructed and Sunday Masses began to be celebrated there. In 1955, the church and shrine were entrusted to the Assumptionists. Also located on the 64 acre property are the Way of the Cross, the Lourdes Grotto, outdoor shrines to St. Anne and Our Lady of Fatima, the Icon Museum and the Holy Stairs. The annual novena to the grandmother of Our Savior takes place July 18-26.

Mailing address: Sturbridge, MA
(6:30 a.m. to 9:00 p.m.)

GLOUCESTER

14. Our Lady of Good Voyage Church: Shrine of the Fisherman, 142 Prospect Street

Situated on Cape Ann, the twin towers and illuminated statue of St. Mary above the church guide the fisherman home. Built in 1915, the house of worship is modeled after a church on the island of San Miguel in the Portugese Azores. A nautical motif can be noted throughout the interior; around the sides and at the choir loft are models of various ships. Over the main altar is a statue of Our Lady of Good Voyage holding a Portugese rigged fishing vessel. Though the church was the first in America to have carillon music, Gloucester is best known for the annual Blessing of the Fleet. After Mass, the bishop leads a procession bearing a replica of Our Lady of Good Voyage to the docks and there blesses the vessels and in memory of those lost at sea, flowers are strewn on the water. *(Open during services only)*

HANOVER

15. *Portiuncula Chapel, Cardinal Cushing School and Training Center*

On the campus of the school for mentally handicapped children, Cardinal Richard Cushing of Boston built a replica of the famous Portiuncula Chapel. (The original was the center of St. Francis of Assisi's activities and the place where the Franciscan order was founded.) The Gothic style chapel with its high arched roof is constructed of pink stones quarried in Carrara, Italy. Built in 1947, the Hanover Portiuncula is now the final resting place of Cardinal Cushing.
(8:30 a.m. to 4:30 p.m.)

HOLLISTON

16. *Our Lady of Fatima Shrine, 101 Summer Street*

Staffed by the Xaverian Missionary Society, the Marian sanctuary was founded in 1950 by Fr. Henry Frassineti. Among its features are Fatima Hill, the Angel of Peace, the Crucifixion Scene, the Grotto of the Pieta and the Scala Sancta (Holy Stairs). The Stations of the Cross are base-reliefs on panels of white translucent marble mounted on rough-faced pillars of Milford pink granite. The shrine has the longest rosary in the world; spread over three acres, it is 950 feet long. On each of the boulder-beads is the Hail Mary inscribed in one of 53 languages.
(Always open)

IPSWICH

17. *National Shrine of Our Lady of La Salette, 315 Topsfield Road.*

Situated on a hilltop 30 miles north of Boston, the shrine contains 350 acres of forest, lawns and gardens. Established in 1945 to commemorate the Blessed Virgin's appearance to two young shepherds in 19th century France, the Marian sanctuary is operated by the La Salette Fathers. The Ipswich haven offers a variety of one day and weekend retreats, workshops and conferences. *(10:00 a.m. to 4:00 p.m.; closed Mon. Oct. to April)*

LEICESTER

18. *Our Lady of Lourdes Grotto, Nazareth Home for Boys, Mulberry Street*

In the fall of 1901, two Sisters of Mercy taking a walk in the nearby woods, located a site which they considered suitable for a grotto. Shortly after, the land was purchased and the sanctuary to Our Lady of Lourdes built. Since 1902, there has been an annual pilgrimage and Mass at the grotto on each August 15, the Feast of the Assumption. Up to 500 people attend the liturgy.

LOWELL

19. *St. Joseph the Worker Shrine, 37 Lee Street*

Having no resident parishioners, St. Joseph's cannot be called a parish. Rather, it is a sacramental shrine in the city's central business district. The picturesque Gothic stone edifice was erected in 1850 to serve a congregation of Unitarians. Sixteen years later, the Oblates of Mary Immaculate purchased it as a spiritual home for the thousands of French Canadians who had come to Lowell seeking employment. Having grown up around the church, Cardinal Cushing of Boston transformed it in 1956 into a "Worker's Shrine" dedicated to St. Joseph. Novenas to the Head of the Holy Family and Bl. Eugene de Mazenod, founder of the Oblates, are on Wednesday at all Masses. *(8:00 a.m. to 6:00 p.m. Sat.; 8:00 a.m. to 12:00 p.m. Sun.)*

STOCKBRIDGE

20. *Shrine of the Divine Mercy, Eden Hill*

In 1931, Our Lord appeared to Sr. Faustina of the Congregation of Sisters of Our Lady of Mercy at their convent in Cracow, Poland. During that and subsequent apparitions, He called for devotion to Divine Mercy. A feast day preceded by a novena was requested and the image and Chaplet of Divine Mercy introduced. The devotion was brought to America by the Marian Fathers who, in 1943, acquired the Eden Hill property as the site for their novitiate. Seven years later, work began on the Shrine of Divine Mercy — a task that would take ten years to accomplish. The Romanesque stone and brick structure was designed by Antonio Guerriri; the stained glass windows are by Fredrich Leuchs. The altar is of Vermont marble; above it is the statue of the Immaculate Conception and behind are wood carvings of the twelve Apostles. To the right and left of the main altar are chapels dedicated to Divine Mercy and St. Joseph. *(6:30 a.m. to 6:00 p.m. M-F; 7:30 a.m. to 6:00 p.m. Sat.; 10:00 a.m. to 6:00 p.m. Sun.)*

WALTHAM

21. *Shrine to the Holy Espousals of the Blessed Virgin Mary and Saint Joseph, Espousal Conference Center, Shrine and Retreat House, 554 Lexington Street*

Located on 60 wooded acres, 12 miles west of Boston, the center is administered by the Stigmatine Fathers. Situated on the grounds is the Espousal Shrine, as well as an indoor shrine containing a colored miniature reproduction of the original. The outdoor shrine consists of three figures sculpted from Carrara marble; represented are the Holy Couple and a Jewish priest at the time of the Espousals of Mary and Joseph.

WORCESTER

22. *Our Lady of Loreto Shrine, Our Lady of Loreto Church, 33 Massasoit Road*

The shrine at Loreto, Italy is said to contain the home of the Holy

Family, which tradition tells us was transported by angels from Nazareth, first to Tersatto, Yugoslavia, then to its present location. Dedicated on August 13, 1989, the Worcester sanctuary is a separate building next to Our Lady of Loreto Church. Designed by Umberto Di Gioia, the shrine's exterior complements the church; inside is a replica of the Holy House. Novenas to the Loreto Madonna are held periodically.

(7:30 a.m. to 3:30 p.m. M-F; 7:30 a.m. to 1:00 p.m. Sun.)

23. St. Anthony's Shrine, 52 High Street

In 1895, a statue of the Franciscan saint was placed in the front hall of the Mercy Sisters' convent. Before long, its popularity was so great that people were constantly ringing the doorbell to leave their petitions or money for candles. Three years later the statue was moved to an outdoor shrine built by Patricia D. Murphy. Located between St. Paul's Cathedral and St. Joseph's Home, the small octagonal wooden shrine is more than ninety-years-old and still popular.

(5:00 a.m. to 5:00 p.m.)

NEW HAMPSHIRE

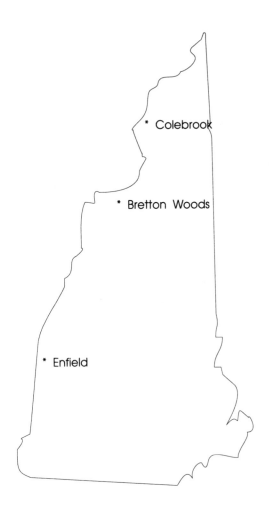

* Colebrook

* Bretton Woods

* Enfield

BRETTON WOODS

24. Our Lady of the Mountains Shrine

The shrine was dedicated on August 15, 1954 by Bishop Matthew Brady of Manchester. A special Mass is held each year on the Feast of the Assumption. One of the best known features of this Marian sanctuary is the portrait of the Blessed Virgin painted by Hungarian artist Bela Szemerei.

Mailing address: c/o St. Matthew Church, 9 Jefferson Road, Whitefield, NH

(June-August only)

COLEBROOK

25. Shrine of Our Lady of Grace, U.S. Highway 3

Situated on 35 acres of landscaped grounds on the Connecticut River near the Canadian border, the shrine had a humble beginning. In 1949, the Oblates of Mary Immaculate, in order to commemorate the 25th anniversary of the Colebrook community, erected an 8-foot white marble statue of the Blessed Virgin Mary mounted on a pedestal of gray Vermont marble. Because of its location near U.S. Route 3, motorists began stopping to admire the memorial and pray. Pilgrims began coming and the Oblates' shrine has become one of the most popular in New England. Among its other attractions are the marble Stations of the Cross, the Family Rosary Pond and the Missionary Rosary. The latter is 300 feet long, each decade is a different color representing five parts of the world and each bead is a flower bed three feet in diameter.

(8:00 a.m. to 5:00 p.m., M-F)

ENFIELD

26. La Salette Shrine and Center, NH Route 4-A

Overlooking Lake Mascoma in the west central part of New Hampshire, the wooded and hilly site of the Marian sanctuary was purchased from a Shaker religious community in 1927. For many years, the La Salette Fathers had a junior house of studies here. The name of their order derives from an incident in 19th century France, in which the Blessed Virgin appeared to two shepherd children and stressed the importance of amending one's life and doing penance. In order to better spread Our Lady's message, the shrine was founded in 1951. Here the story of the La Salette apparition is told by hillside sculptures and by the lovely stained glass windows of the Renaissance chapel. Among the other attractions of the shrine are the life-size Way of the Cross, the Calvery Group, the Rosary Pond and the Peace Walk. During Advent, thousands of lights illuminate the sanctuary's special Christmas displays. During the summer Marian devotions are held each Sunday afternoon.

(Always open)

NEW JERSEY

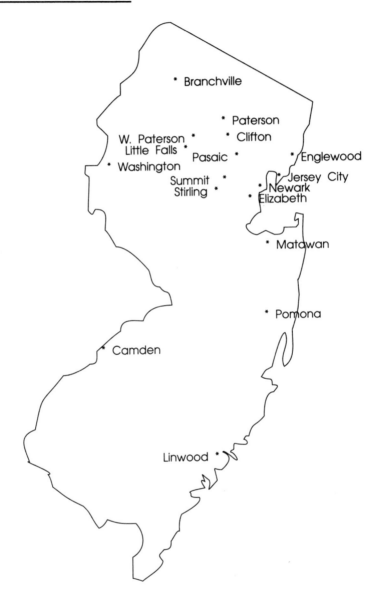

* Branchville

* Paterson
W. Paterson * * Clifton
Little Falls *
* Pasaic * * Englewood
* Washington
Summit * * Jersey City
Stirling * * Newark
* Elizabeth

* Matawan

* Pomona

* Camden

Linwood *

BRANCHVILLE

27. Sanctuary of Mary, Our Lady of the Holy Spirit, NJ Route 519

The 23 acre spiritual haven in the Kittatinny Mountains was founded in 1972 by Fr. Sylvester Livolsi. Not a shrine in the Western sense but rather an Eastern style *Poustina*, the sanctuary is very much a place of pilgrimage. Here the Fraternitas (Sororitas) Mariana Spiritus, a new diocesan order of Brothers and Sisters, has its headquarters, and the canonization of Sister Miriam Therese Demjanovich, S.C. is promoted.

(Always open)

CAMDEN

28. Our Lady's Perpetual Rosary Shrine, Monastery of the Perpetual Rosary, 1500 Haddon Avenue

The Dominican Nun's shrine is the headquarters of the Perpetual Rosary Association and is famous for the rare paintings depicting the mysteries of the rosary in the chapel.

CLIFTON

29. Holy Face Monastery, 1697 Rt. S-3

Staffed by the Sylvestrine Benedictine Monks, the monastery is a center of devotion to the Holy Face of Jesus and disseminates information regarding the Shroud of Turin. A life-size replica of the Holy Shroud is displayed to help pilgrims better visualize the suffering and death of Our Savior.

(6:30 a.m. to 8:00 p.m.)

ELIZABETH

30. Sts. Peter and Paul Roman Catholic Church, 211 Ripley Place

The Shrine at Siluva where the Blessed Virgin appeared in 1608, is Lithuania's most popular Marian sanctuary. In 1958, under the direction of Fr. Michael G. Kemezis a shrine honoring Our Lady of Siluva was erected in the church at Elizabeth. Ornamented with Lithuanian art work and wood carvings, it has a painting portraying the apparition and a relic of the original stone on which Our Lady stood.

(Open during services only)

ENGLEWOOD

31. St. Cecilia's Church and Priory, 55 Demerest Avenue
The Eastern Shrine of the Little Flower was established by Fr. Albert H. Dolan, the foremost U.S. apostle of St. Therese of Lisieux and founder of the Society of the Little Flower. The Carmelite Church has important relics of the saint. Since the 1930s people have been coming here to pray and attend devotions to the Saint of the Little Way. *(7:30 a.m. to 4:00 p.m. M-S; 8:00 a.m. to 4:00 p.m. Sun.)*

JERSEY CITY

32. Shrine of St. Jude, St. Michael Church, 252 Ninth Street
Every Tuesday there are seven novena services in honor of the Saint of the Impossible at this popular shrine. *(Open during services only)*

LINWOOD

33. Shrine of Our Lady of Sorrows and of All Consolation, Our Lady of Sorrows Church, 200 Wilson Avenue
The Missionaries of the Sacred Hearts of Jesus and Mary who staff this church have a special devotion to Our Lady of Sorrows. So it should come as no surprise that their only parish in the U.S. is named in her honor. There is a novena to the Sorrowful Mother each Friday morning. *(Open during services only)*

LITTLE FALLS

34. National Shrine of Our Lady of the Highway, Our Lady of Holy Angels Church, 473 Main Street
In 1939, after being involved in a tragic automobile accident, Fr. Giles Lawlor revived the ancient devotion to the *Madonna della Strada* in the Franciscan church in the Singac section of Little Falls. With permission of the bishop of Patterson, a medal was struck. Next to the church is the campanile with its three bells and Our Lady of the Highway in repousse.

MATAWAN

35. Basilian Fathers of Mariapoch Monastery, 360 Monastery Lane

Mariapoch is one of the most important Marian sanctuaries in Hungary. Its revered image of the Blessed Mother is said to have wept on two occasions: 1715 and 1905. Especially esteemed by Catholics of the Byzantine Rite, the shrine is administered by the Basilian Fathers. In 1964, priests of that order established a monastery in Matawan. The Hungarian priests have a replica of the weeping Madonna at their New Jersey home. Each year there is a pilgrimage in honor of Our Lady of Mariapoch.
(8:00 a.m. to 8:00 p.m.)

NEWARK

36. National Shrine of St. Gerard, St. Lucy's Church, 118 Seventh Avenue

St. Gerard Majella, the son of a tailor in southern Italy, joined the Redemptorist as a lay brother in 1748. Four years later, he was professed by St. Alphonsus Ligouri, founder of the order. Soon his supernatural gifts — bilocation, prophecy, ecstacies, visions and infused knowledge — became apparent to all. He was also known for his holiness and charity, and for his success in converting sinners. He died in Caposele in 1755. Since many of the parishioners of St. Lucy's Church came from that Italian city, they are devoted to him. In 1977, the National Council of Catholic Bishops declared the church to be the National Shrine of St. Gerard. Each year since 1899, his feast is celebrated, the culmination of nine days of prayer in his honor. For three days his statue is carried through the streets in procession. St. Gerard is the patron of motherhood; it is said that many previously barren women have conceived after making a novena or walking in procession.
(7:00 a.m. to 3:00 p.m. M-F; 7:00 a.m. to 7:00 p.m. Sat.; 7:30 a.m. to 2:00 p.m. Sun.)

37. Stella Maris Chapel, 114 Corbin Avenue (Port Newark)

Located on the bayside of Newark, the chapel boasts a painting of St. Mary, Star of the Sea and daily novenas in her honor. Each year more than 10,000 people visit this center of devotion. Also at this location is Vercelli Institute which offers courses in Philosophy and Theology.

Mailing address: c/o St. James Rectory, 143 Madison Street, Newark, NJ
(9:00 a.m. to 4:30 p.m. M-F; 9:00 a.m. to 9:00 p.m. Sat.; 9:00 a.m. to 1:00 p.m. Sun.)

PATERSON

38. St. Bonaventure Church, 174 Ramsey Street
Adjacent to St. Bonaventure Friary, the Franciscan church founded in 1877 is a center of devotion to St. Anthony. Novenas to the saint from Padua are held each Tuesday.
(7:00 a.m. to 7:30 p.m. M-F; 8:00 a.m. to 6:00 p.m. Sat.; 7:30 a.m. to 5:30 p.m. Sun.)

POMONA

39. Shrine of Our Lady of the Highway, Sea and Air, Church of the Assumption, 1993 White Horse Pike
Located on U.S. Route 30, 14 miles from Atlantic City, the Marian sanctuary is popular with many South Jersey motorists. Candles burn day and night, attesting to the love and devotion of many travelers who stop to pray. The outdoor shrine consists of a statue of Our Lady of the Way in a three-sided enclosure with a roof supported by three fluted arches.

STIRLING

40. Shrine of St. Joseph, 1050 Long Hill Road
Located in the Watchung Mountains, the site was purchased in 1924 by Fr. Thomas A. Judge, founder of the Missionary Servants of the Most Holy Trinity. Its first use was as a place for weekend retreats for young men. Two years later, a group of boys, with Fr. Judge's encouragement, erected an outdoor statue of St. Joseph here. It proved so popular that a chapel was built to house it in 1928. The shrine was completely rebuilt in the 1970's under the direction of Fr. Leonard Boehmann. In addition to the new St. Joseph Chapel, there

are outdoor shrines to Our Lady of Humility, St. Anthony, Mother Cabrini, St. Anne, the Holy Cross, St. Martin de Porres, and Our Lady of Fatima. There is also the Hall of the Saints, the Way of the Cross and the original shrine chapel. Devotions in honor of St. Joseph are conducted every Sunday afternoon.
(7:00 a.m. to 9:00 p.m.)

SUMMIT

41. Rosary Shrine, Monastery of Our Lady of the Rosary, 543 Springfield Avenue

In 1926, the privilege of perpetual exposition of the Blessed Sacrament was granted to this monastery. Ever since, hour after hour, cloistered Dominican nuns have succeeded each other in reciting the Eucharistic Rosary, before the magnificent marble Altar of Repose in the monastery's Gothic chapel. Also, on the grounds is a shrine dedicated to Our Lady of Fatima. On Sundays and Marian Holy Days and throughout May and October, pilgrims come from all over the East. One of the Sisters' proudest possessions is a copy of the Shroud of Turin given them by the Dominican Nuns of St. Dominic and St. Sixtus Monastery in Rome in whose possession it had been for 300 years. The replica had been made in 1624 at the command of the Grand Duchess of Austria.
(9:00 a.m. to 4:00 p.m. M-F; 1:00 p.m. to 4:00 p.m. Sun.)

WASHINGTON

42. Shrine of the Immaculate Heart of Mary, Mountain View Road

Built in 1978, the Marian sanctuary also serves as the national headquarters of the Blue Army of Fatima. Standing on the single crowned tower, 145 feet in height, the bronze statue of Our Lady dominates the shrine. But its spiritual heart is Our Eucharistic Lord present in the Blessed Sacrament Chapel on the lower level. Also on the grounds are the Rosary Gardens, Holy House, U.S.A., the Capelinha and the outdoor Stations of the Cross. The Capelinha is a replica of the chapel at Fatima built in 1921 on the site of the famous apparitions. Holy House, U.S.A., built in 1973 and staffed by the Handmaids of Mary Immaculate, has the same dimensions as that in which the Holy Family lived. (The original is said to have been transported from Nazareth to Loreto, Italy by angels). Sister Lucia's last vision — at Tuy — is depicted in statuary in the chapel of the Holy House, U.S.A. Pilgrims may also visit the Padre Pio monument and outdoor shrines honoring Our Lady of Kazan, St. Anne, Our Lady of Perpetual Help, St. Therese, Our Lady of Czestochowa, St. Francis, and the Angel of Peace.

(Shrine: 11:00 a.m. to 4:30 p.m.; Holy House: 9:30 a.m. to 6:00 p.m.)

WEST PATERSON

43. Our Lady of America Shrine, St. Anne's Melkite Catholic Church, 802 Rifle Camp Road

The icon of Our Lady of America was commissioned in 1976 to symbolize the rededication of the United States to the Mother of God on the occasion of our nation's bicentennial. Painted on wood and covered with a jeweled shield, it depicts the Blessed Mother and the Child Jesus. The icon has been solemnly blessed by His Beatitude Maximos V. Hakim, Patriarch of Antioch and worldwide head of the Melkite Catholic Church.

(Open during services only)

NEW YORK

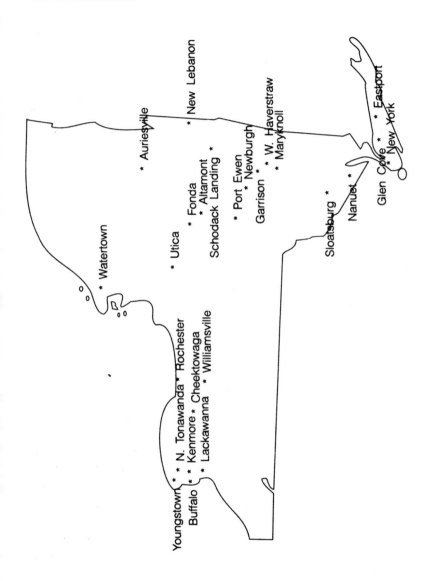

ALTAMONT

44. La Salette Shrine, Leesome Lane

One of several such sanctuaries scattered throughout the country, the shrine operated by the La Salette Fathers commemorates the apparition of the Blessed Mother to two French shepherd children on September 19, 1846.
(9:00 a.m. to 4:40 p.m.)

AURIESVILLE

45. National Shrine of the North American Martyrs, Intersection of NY Routes 5-S and 288

Auriesville is the site of the Mohawk village of Ossernenon, said to be the birthplace of Bl. Kateri Tekakwitha. It was here in August, 1642 that the Jesuits Fr. Isaac Jogues and Br. Rene Goupil, both newly arrived from France, were brought after being captured by the Indians. The following month, Br. Rene was martyred after being observed making the sign of the cross over a Mohawk youth. Though cruelly tortured, Fr. Jogues escaped a year later. After recovering from the ordeal, the Jesuit priest accompanied by Br. John La Lande returned to Ossernenon. There the two met their deaths on October 18 and 19, 1646. The three heroic victims, together with five Jesuit missionaries martyred in Canada were canonized in 1960. The Shrine of the North American Martyrs in the Mohawk Valley, near Albany is operated by the Jesuit province of New York. The first public pilgrimage was made in 1885. The small oratory erected then soon proved too small. A rustic chapel, open on three sides and seating 500 people was built nine years later. This, in turn, gave way to the Coliseum Church dedicated in 1931. Built to accommodate 6,500 worshipers, the buff-colored brick structure was one of the first circular churches in the United States. The altar of the Coliseum was built to resemble log palisades which usually surrounded Mohawk villages. Among the attractions of the shrine is the Way of the Cross which leads to a Calvary group atop a hill where Fr. Jogues and Br. Goupil prayed during their days of captivity. The Martyrs Museum adjacent to the church houses important relics of the missionaries and their Indian converts. Scattered throughout the

grounds are small shrines honoring St. Isaac Jogues, Our Lady of Fatima, Bl. Kateri Tekakwitha, and St. Rene Goupil. A replica of the famous Pieta is housed in a picturesque outdoor chapel. Open first Sunday in May to last Sunday in October.
(11:00 a.m. to 5:00 p.m. M-S; 9:00 a.m. to 5:00 p.m. Sun.)

BROOKLYN

46. Shrine Church of St. Bernadette, 8201 13th Avenue

One of two Brooklyn churches sponsoring devotions to Our Lady of Lourdes, the 13th Avenue Shrine is dedicated to the visionary of Massabielle. The Marian sanctuary has indoor and outdoor grottos in honor of St. Bernadette's Virgin. In addition to weekly novenas there is an annual celebration in honor of Our Lady of Lourdes.
(6:30 a.m. to 5:00 p.m. M-F; 6:30 a.m. to 5:30 p.m. Sat.; 9:30 a.m. to 5:30 p.m. Sun.)

47. Our Lady of Lourdes Church, 89 Furman Avenue

In 1897, the Fathers of Mercy under the rectorship of Fr. Eugene Porcile built a new classic Romanesque structure on the site formerly occupied by St. Francis de Sales Church. The church, famous for its shrine to St. Bernadette's Lady, burned in 1973. It has been replaced by a small chapel and grotto. On the third Sunday of each month, afternoon devotions to Our Lady of Lourdes feature a candlelight procession and Benediction.

Mailing address: 11 De Sales Place, Brooklyn, NY
(Open during services only)

48. Shrine of Our Lady of Mt. Carmel, 275 North 8th Street

To accommodate the large number of Italian immigrants who had settled in the Williamsburg section of Brooklyn, the Mt. Carmel parish was established in 1887. The present church (the third) was built in 1950. The shrine is famous for its annual feast in honor of Our Lady of Mt. Carmel and St. Paulinas of Nola. The celebration lasts more than a week and features a candlelight procession, nightly novenas (in English and Italian) and the dancing of the Giglio and Boat. The tradition is more than 100-years-old.
(Open during services only)

49. Basilica of Our Lady of Perpetual Help, 526 Fifty-Ninth Street

Raised to the rank of a minor Basilica on September 5, 1969, the Redemptionist church continues to follow Pope Pius IX's order to propagate devotion to Our Lady of Perpetual Help.
(Open during services only)

50. Our Lady of Solace Shrine Church, 2866 West 17th Street

Pope Pius X granted this Coney Island church the title of Roman Shrine with the Portuncula Indulgence for those who visit and pray for the holy Souls.
(Always open)

51. Regina Pacis Votive Shrine, 1230-65th Street

During world war II, to obtain the safe return of the soldiers and a just peace, the parishioners of St. Rosalia's Church vowed to build a shrine in honor of Our Lady, Queen of Peace. Nine years later, in 1951, the completed Marian sanctuary was dedicated by Archbishop Thomas E. Mulloy of Brooklyn. The facade of the church is impressive with its Massive bronze doors, large rose window and statue of Regina Pacis. The adjoining Indiana limestone belfry is 150 feet in height. Inside, on the altar throne is the famous painting by Ilario Panzironi of Our Lady, Queen of Peace with her Divine Son. In 1954, two diamond studded crowns blessed by Pope Pius XII were bestowed on Regina Pacis and Child. Though stolen only nine days later, the symbols of royalty were miraculously returned within a week.
(9:00 a.m. to 6:00 p.m.)

52. St. Rita's Church, 275 Shepard Avenue

The church is the site of an annual novena to the saint from Cascia, Italy, patroness of difficult cases.
(Opening during services only)

BUFFALO

53. Shrine of St. Jude, St. Stephen's Roman Catholic Church, 193 Elk Street

Under the directorship of Fr. Edwin J. Kaukus, St. Stephen's is the official St. Jude shrine of the diocese of Buffalo. Three devotions

in honor of the Sacred Heart of Jesus and the Saint of Difficult Cases are conducted every Friday. Also, there is an Annual Solemn Novena to St. Jude Thaddeus October 20th to 28th.
(9:00 a.m. to 5:00 p.m)

54. National Shrine of the Little Flower of Jesus, Carmelite Monastery, 75 Carmel Road

In 1920, at the invitation of Fr. Nelson Baker and Bishop Willian Turner, a small community of exiled Discalced Carmelite Nuns from Mexico under the leadership of Mother Mary Elias of the Blessed Sacrament arrived in Buffalo and established a monastery on Cottage Street. With the encouragement of Fr. George A. Crimmen, their chaplain, the sisters' modest chapel soon developed into a center of veneration of the Little Flower. To accommodate the many pilgrims and the community's many new vocations, a new chapel and monastery were built on Carmel Road in 1925. It was dedicated on the same day that St. Therese of Lisieux was canonized and is known as her national shrine.
(8:30 a.m. to 5:30 p.m.)

CHEEKTOWAGA

55. Our Lady, Help of Christians Chapel, 4125 Union Road

In 1836, on his way from Alsace to his new home in America, Joseph Batt was caught in a storm at sea. Realizing his danger, he placed himself and his family in the Blessed Mother's hands, promising that if they survived, he would build a chapel in her honor. Seventeen years later, with the encouragement of St. John Neumann, he fulfilled his vow when the cornerstone of the "Maria Hilf" shrine was laid. The Marian sanctuary was immediately popular with the many German-speaking immigrants in the Buffalo area, so in 1871 Batt had to expand the stone chapel. As the population of Cheektowaga increased, Our Lady, Help of Christians became a parish. Pilgrims continued to come, especially on May 24 and August 15. The chapel was enlarged again in 1926. Thirty-three years later, a new larger church was built. Though the old chapel fell into disuse for a while, it was restored in 1976 as a bicentennial project. Two years later, the Cheektowaga shrine was placed on the

list of National Historical Sites. The chapel is still used for Masses, Holy Hours and Marian devotions.
(Open during services only)

EASTPORT

56. Shrine of Our Lady of the Island, Eastport Manor Road

Atop the largest rock formation on Long Island stands an 18-foot statue of the Blessed Mother and the Child Jesus overlooking Moriches Bay and the Atlantic Ocean. The 22-ton image of Our Lady was designed by Raphael De Sota and sculpted out of Vermont granite by Fran Marchini. Also of interest at the 60-plus-acres haven administered by the Montfort Fathers are the Stations of the Cross with its life size Calvary scene, the Blessed Sacrament Chapel and the Rosary Walk. In the latter, a giant cross cut from Evergreen guards the entrance and 150 Juniper bushes spaced in a quarter mile circle mark off each Hail Mary.
(9:00 a.m. to 4:00 p.m.)

ELMIRA

57. Shrine of Our Lady, Queen of Peace, Mount Savior Monastery

In the crypt of the monastery church of this independent Benedictine community is the shrine of Our Lady, Queen of Peace. The object of veneration is a 14th century School of Paris stone statue of the Blessed Virgin Mary. Since its founding in 1951, the monastery has been a center of pilgrimages and retreats.

Mailing address: Pine City, NY
(4:45 a.m. to 8:30 p.m.)

FONDA

58. National Shrine of Blessed Kateri Tekakwitha, Route 5

Born in 1656, the "Lily of the Mohawks" had a pagan father and a Christian mother. When she was three-years-old, smallpox struck her village killing her parents. Kateri survived but with a pock marked face and poor eyesight. After the destruction of her home, she moved to the Indian Village of Caughnawaga where she was baptized in 1676 in St. Peter's Church, in spite of her uncle's

objections. After much persecution the new Christian escaped to
Kahnawake, Canada. There she lived a life of holiness and penance.
In 1679 she took a vow of perpetual virginity; the following year she
died. The national shrine was established in 1938 and is staffed by
the Conventual Franciscans. The staked out Indian village where
Kateri Tekakwitha spent almost half of her life is on the grounds. It
was discovered by Fr. Thomas Grassman, the founder and first
director of the shrine. Nearby is Mohawk-Caughnawaga Museum
and St. Peter's Chapel, named after the place of her baptism.
(May 15 to October 15 only; 10:00 a.m. to 4:00 p.m.)

GARRISON

59. Graymoor, NY Route 9

Located on the Hudson, forty miles north of New York City,
Graymoor is the home of the Society of the Atonement. Its founders,
Paul Wattson and Lurana Mary White were Episcopalians who
sought to live the religious life according to the rule of St. Francis.
Also among their objectives was the corporate reunion of the
Anglican and Roman Catholic churches. They inaugurated the
Chair of Unity Octave which has evolved into the Week of Prayer
for Christian Unity. In 1909 the entire society entered the Catholic
Church; shortly afterward Wattson was ordained as a Roman
Catholic priest. Over the years the Franciscan Friars and Sisters of
the Atonement have grown considerably. Located on the grounds
of Graymoor are St. Christopher's Inn, Matt Talbot Hall, the
Shrine of Our Lady of the Atonement and the Tombs of Fr. Paul
and Mother Lurana. The Inn is a place of shelter for the homeless,
while the Hall is an alcoholic rehabilitation center.
(9:00 a.m. to 4:00 p.m.)

GLEN COVE

60. St. Josephat Monastery, East Beach Dr.

This Byzantine Rite monastery is the novitiate house of the
Basilian Fathers. Each year Ukranian Catholics from New York and
Long Island make a pilgrimage here.
(7:30 a.m. to 5:30 p.m. M-S; 9:30 a.m. to 5:30 p.m. Sun.)

KENMORE

61. Shrine of St. John Neumann, St. John the Baptist Church, 1085 Englewood Avenue

The western New York parish was founded in 1836 by St. John Neumann who also served as its first pastor. St. John the Baptist has grown since that time and is now the largest in the diocese. The founder's log church was replaced by a Romanesque stone structure in 1856, and then by another chapel in 1899. This latter, now restored chapel, serves as the shrine to St. John Neumann. A nine day solemn novena leading up to the anniversary of the canonization of St. John Neumann is conducted each year in June.
(2:00 a.m. to 4:00 p.m. M-F)

LACKAWANNA

62. Our Lady of Bistrica Croatian Roman Catholic Church, 1619 Abbot Road

In 1545 refugees from Vinski Vrh brought their treasured madonna to Bistrica for safekeeping. There it remained until 1684 when a series of miracles brought national attention to the darkened with age wooden statue. Twenty-six years later, a great shrine was built in her honor by order of the Croatian Parliament. In 1935, Our Lady of Bistrica was crowned as Queen of Croatia. The Lackawanna church serves as her shrine in America.
(Open during services only)

63. Our Lady of Victory Basilica and National Shrine, South Park Avenue and Ridge Road

After achieving success in business, Nelson H. Baker gave up the world of commerce to enter the seminary. During a subsequent trip to Paris, he visited the Church of Our Lady of Victory where he dedicated his life to its patroness and promised to one day build a shrine in her honor in America. In 1876, the newly ordained Fr. Baker was sent to Lackawanna to assist in the operation of a nearly bankrupt orphanage. There he formed the Association of Our Lady of Victory to raise funds. So successful was he that he was made superintendent of what was destined to be Our Lady of Victory Homes of Charity, with its orphanage, industrial school, home for

infants, facilities for unwed mothers and maternity hospital. Later Fr. Baker became Vicar General of the diocese of Buffalo. In 1921, at age eighty, he began construction of the National Shrine of Our Lady of Victory. Five years later, after the expenditure of three and a half million dollars, the elegant Italian Renaissance structure was completed. A great dome and flanking towers mark its exterior, while inside all eyes gravitate toward the main altar with its twisted columns of rare Pyrenese red marble. Dominating it is the nine foot, 1,600 pound statue of Our Lady of Victory. Two months after its completion Pope Pius XI elevated the shrine to a minor basilica, making it the second such church in the United States. In the summer of 1987, the Vatican opened the cause for the canonization of Fr. Nelson Baker.
(7:30 a.m. to 7:30 p.m.)

MARYKNOLL

64. Maryknoll Center
Located near Ossining is the seminary and headquarters of the Catholic Foreign Mission Society. Each year a new group of missionaries leaves here after an impressive departure ceremony. Founded in 1911 by Bishop James A. Walsh and Fr. Thomas F. Price, the Society has nearly one thousand priests, brothers and lay missioners serving in twenty-seven lands. The crypt where the two co-founders are buried and a museum dedicated to them may be visited by the public. Pilgrims may also view the shrine of Our Lady of Maryknoll which features a sculpture of the Madonna and Child housed in a red kiosk of Chinese design. Also of interest is the departure bell, which originally hung in a Buddhist monastery; the Chapel of Mary, Queen of Martyrs; and the Society Library containing 96,000 volumes devoted to the missions. The motherhouse of the Maryknoll Sisters of St. Dominic is nearby.
(8:00 a.m. to 5:00 p.m. Sat. and Sun.)

NANUET

65. St. Anthony's Shrine Church, 38 East Route 59A
Originally located in Bardonia, the church was relocated to nearby Nanuet after the tragic fire of 1912. Completed eight years

later, the modified country Gothic house of worship obtained true relics of the Wonder Worker of Padua obtained from Rome in 1923. These were enshrined in a beautiful new chapel. The newly organized League of St. Anthony enrolled members nationwide. Pilgrims flocked to the shrine during the summer months. In 1969, work began on a new larger church.

(8:00 a.m. to 7:00 p.m.)

NEW LEBANON

66. Our Lady of Lourdes Grotto, Immaculate Conception Church, U.S. Route 20

Under the direction of Dr. John Le Fevre, the people of this parish built the Lourdes shrine using native stone from the New Lebanon Valley. Dedicated in 1929, the outdoor sanctuary is unusual in its design. From the lovely statue of Our Lady in her niche well back in the center of the grotto, five arches progressively increasing in size form the roof and sides of the shrine.

NEW YORK

67. Shrine of St. Ann, St. Jean Baptiste Church, 184 East 76th Street

Founded in 1882 by Fr. Charles De La Croix, St. Jean was intended to serve as a national parish for the French and French Canadians of New York's East Side. Ten years later, a Monsignor from Rome enroute to the shrine at Beaupre, Quebec arrived. On learning that he was bearing relics of St. Ann, a gift from Pope Leo XIII, the pastor asked that they be exposed for veneration by his parishioners. The results were sensational; many miracles took place and for three weeks pilgrims from every part of the country thronged to the church. Moved by this display of fevor, the bearer of the relic upon arriving at the French Canadian shrine requested that the object of devotion be divided. The request was honored and a portion of the relic returned to New York. The first annual novena to St. Ann began on July 17, 1892. Eight years later, the Blessed Sacrament Fathers were given charge of St. Jean Baptiste. By 1912, the shrine having become too small, construction of a new Classical-Renaissance structure began. The shrine is now located in the crypt of the church.

Mailing address: Saint Ann's Shrine, Blessed Sacrament Fathers, 5384 Wilson Mills Road, Cleveland, OH
(7:00 a.m. to 7:00 p.m. M-F; 8:30 a.m. to 7:00 p.m. Sat.; 8:30 a.m. to 8:30 p.m. Sun.)

68. National Shrine of the Motherhood of St. Ann, St. Ann's Church, 110 East 12th Street

Originally located on Astor Place, the church, prior to its acquisition by the Archdiocese of New York, was occupied successively by Presbyterians, Episcopalians, and Swedenborgians. The new East 12th Street Church, purchased in 1862, has a similar history: it has been a Baptist house of worship and a Jewish synagogue. The popular novena preceding the feast of St. Ann was inaugurated in 1915 by Fr. John J. Southwick. A confraternity devoted to the Grandmother of Jesus was formed. In 1929, the Vatican declared the church to be America's National Shrine of the Motherhood of Saint Ann and the Primary Church of the confraternity in the United States. The church's interior was constructed in the 13th-century French Gothic style. To the right of the sanctuary is the shrine of the church's patroness, its focus is an impressive Carrara marble statue of St. Ann, shown gazing down at her daughter Mary.
(11:30 a.m. to 2:00 p.m. M-F; 3:00 p.m. to 6:00 p.m. Sat.; 10:00 a.m. to 1:00 p.m. Sun.)

69. National Shrine of St. Anthony, Church of St. Francis of Assisi, 135 West 3lst Street

One of the most beloved saints of all times, St. Anthony was born in Portugal toward the end of the 12th century. Joining the Franciscans in 1221, he became noted for his piety, eloquence and learning. He died 10 years later. An old legend has it that one day a friar entered St. Anthony's cell unannounced. The room was ablaze with light and the saint, oblivious to everything else, was seen holding the Divine Child in his arms. Since 1930, the National Shrine of the Saint from Padua has been housed in the crypt of this Franciscan Church. There are weekly novenas in his honor. St.

Monica, mother of St. Augustine, is also popular here. There is an annual week of prayer in her honor and four novena services each Monday.
(6:45 a.m. to 7:00 p.m.)

70. Mother Cabrini Chapel, Cabrini high School, 701 Fort Washington Avenue

Called the Patroness of Immigrants, the Italian-born St. Frances Cabrini was the foundress of the Missionary Sisters of the Sacred heart. In 1889, at the request of Pope Leo XIII she came to the United States to render spiritual and charitable assistance to the many sons and daughters of Italy in America. The next twenty-eight years prior to her death in Chicago's Columbus hospital, were spent founding hospitals, schools, convents and orphanages and performing other works of charity. Canonized in 1946, she was the first American citizen so honored. Mother Cabrini's remains are enclosed in a crystal coffin under the main altar of the chapel.
(9:00 a.m. to 4:30 p.m.; Closed Mon.)

71. St. Joseph of the Holy Family Church, 405 West 125th Street

The church is popular among New York's Black Catholics as a center of devotion to the Martyrs of Uganda. In 1964, St. Charles Lwanga, St. Joseph Mkasa and 20 other companion martyrs were canonized by Pope Paul VI as the high point of his journey to Africa.
(Open during services only)

72. Shrine of St. Jude, Church of St. Stephen of Hungary, 414 East 82nd Street

The Franciscan Friars who staff the church conduct a perpetual novena to the Saint of the Impossible each Wednesday at 9:00, 3:00 and 7:00 p.m. In addition, there are Solemn Novenas each year in January, April, August and October.
(9:00 a.m. to 5:30 p.m.)

73. Dominican Shrine of St. Jude, St. Catherine of Siena Church, 411 East 68th Street

The Order of Preachers also has a sanctuary to the Patron of Difficult Cases in the nation's largest city. Though more petitioners

are presented via the mails than in person, there is a St. Jude novena before the 5:15 p.m. Mass each day. The Dominicans hold eight Solemn Novenas a year; in seven of these the saint is paired with another. The other holy persons so honored are: the Infant of Prague, St. Jude, St. Catherine of Siena, the Sacred Heart, St. Anne, Our Lady of Fatima and the Immaculate Conception. The specific dates for these novenas, except St. Jude Thaddeus' vary each year. The novena of Masses to the Shrine's patron saint is from September 1st to the 9th. The church also has an authenticated relic of St. Jude which is venerated each Friday.
(6:00 a.m. to 6:00 p.m.)

74. St. Lucy's Church, 833 Mace Avenue (Bronx)

For many years the church has been noted for its Lourdes Grotto and its Scala Santa. St. Lucy's parishioners are Italian Americans.
(Open during services only)

75. Notre Dame Church, 405 West 114th Street

Founded in 1911 as a French national parish, the Morningside Heights church has become a center of devotion to the Virgin of St. Bernadette. Designed on the pattern of the Invalides in Paris, the Marian sanctuary has a statue of Our Lady of Lourdes above and a grotto behind the main altar. There are weekly novenas and an annual feast day celebration in honor of the church's patroness.
(Open during services only)

76. Our Lady of Guadalupe Church, 229 West 14th Street

Called the Mother Church of the Spanish-speaking people of the nation's largest city, Our Lady of Guadalupe, founded in 1902, was the first parish established to serve their spiritual needs. Staffed by the Augustinians of the Assumption, it remains the city's largest and most popular Hispanic church.
(7:30 a.m. to 7:30 p.m. M-S; 9:00 a.m. to 7:00 p.m. Sun.)

77. Our Lady of Mt. Carmel Church and Shrine, 448 East 116th Street

Administered by the priests of the Society of the Catholic Apostolate, better known as the Pallottine Fathers, the East Harlem

shrine's miraculous statue of Our Lady of Mt. Carmel has been
venerated here for more than 100 years. In 1904, the revered image
was incoronated with the consent of Pope Pius X. (Ten years earlier,
Pope Leo XIII had granted a plenary indulgence to all who
participate in the devotions at the ll6th Street church.) The shrine has
remained popular; thousands of people from near and far visit the
church each year in July, especially on the I6th — the feast of Our
Lady of Mt. Carmel. There is a perpetual novena to the Madonna of
the Scapular each Wednesday at 9:00 a.m. in Italian and 7:30 p.m. in
English.
(9:00 a.m. to 5:00 p.m.; stop at rectory first)

78. Shrine-Church of Our Lady of Pompeii, 25 Carmine Street

In 1873, Bl. Barto Longo obtained a painting featuring Our Lady
of the Rosary, St. Dominic and St. Catherine of Siena for his newly
established confraternity group. The picture was placed in a local
chapel and before long reports of miracles were heard. The shrine
subsequently built became one of Italy's most famous pilgrimage
centers. To serve immigrants from that country, the Greenwich
Village church overlooking Demo Square was built in 1928.
Designed by Matteo Dei Guadio and staffed by the Scalabrinian
Fathers, the magnificent classical house of worship has become a
center for propagating devotion to Our Lady of the Rosary. The
shrine even has its own radio program for this purpose. The church
itself is a work of art with its paintings of the mysteries of the rosary,
its ornate columns and its giant mural above its sanctuary. Atop its
lovely altar is a painting of Our Lady of Pompeii.
*(6:00 a.m. to 1:00 p.m. M-F; 7:30 a.m. to 10:00 a.m. and 4:00 p.m.
to 6:00 p.m. Sat.; 8:00 a.m. to 10:30 a.m. Sun.)*

79. Our Lady of the Scapular of Mt. Carmel Church, 339 East 28th Street

Built in 1889 to serve the spiritual needs of the Irish Catholics of
the area, the church is administered by the Carmelites. Above the
main altar, covering the entire wall, is a mural portraying Our Lady
of Mt. Carmel giving the Brown Scapular to St. Simon Stock painted
by Ariel Agemian. The stained glass windows depict the history of

the Carmelite Order. There is an annual novena in honor of the Virgin of Mt. Carmel.
(Open during services only)

80. Padre Pio Prayer Garden, St. John's Church, 210 West 31st Street

Located across from Madison Square Garden and Penn Station in Manhattan, the Capuchins have created a haven of quiet and serenity on the church grounds. The garden has a life-size marble statue of Padre Pio and four bronze plaques depicting scenes from his life. There is a monthly holy hour for the beatification of the Capuchin stigmatic, consisting of Rosary, Mass and sermon conducted by Fr. Armand Dasseville.
(8:00 a.m. to 6:00 p.m. M-S; 8:00 a.m. to 1:00 p.m. Sun.)

81. St. Paul's Church, 113 East 117th Street

In 1876, after the Blessed Virgin appeared to the terminaly ill Estelle Faguette, the visionary of Provolision, France was miraculously cured of Tuberculosis. In all there were fifteen apparitions. During one, the Blessed Mother gave the world the Scapular of the Sacred Heart. The latter has been approved by the church and the Confraternity of Mary, Mother of Mercy established. Founded in 1837, St. Paul's Church in East Harlem has the only public shrine to Our Lady of Provolision in the United States. It was erected in 1935 by Fr. Thomas F. Kane, upon returning from a pilgrimage to the principal Marian sanctuaries of France. Novenas to the French Madonna are still held here.
(Open during services only)

82. St. Peter's Church, 16 Barclay Street

With financial assistance from the Spanish ambassador, the church was officially opened in 1786, making it the oldest church in New York City. Partially destroyed by fire during an anti-papist riot in the 1830's, a new Classical Greek style church was built in 1844. It was here that Elizabeth Ann Seton, the first native born American saint and foundress of the Sisters of Charity received her First Communion in 1805. A year later she was confirmed at St. Peter's by Archbishop Carroll of Baltimore, America's first bishop. Because of the distance between the church and her home, Mother Seton often spent the whole day at church, having breakfast after Mass with one group of friends, her dinner with another, and finally returning home after Vespers. Another parishioner was Pierre Touissant, the black ex-slave from Haiti and candidate for canonization.

(7:00 a.m. to 6:00 p.m. M-S; 8:00 a.m. to 1:00 p.m. Sun.)

83. Schoenstatt Shrine, 337 Carey Avenue, Staten Island

The Staten Island Marian sanctuary is one of over 80 scattered throughout the world. Each is a replica of the original shrine of the Mother Thrice Admirable, Queen and Victoress of Schoenstatt, Germany. Dedicated in 1977, the New York shrine is under the care of the Schoenstatt Sisters of Mary.

(8:00 a.m. to 8:30 p.m.)

84. Shrine of St. Elizabeth Ann Seton, Church of Our Lady of the Rosary and Seton Residence, 708 State Street

Situated opposite Battery Park at the tip of Manhattan Island, this was the home of the New York born saint and her family from 1801 to 1803. The State Street residence and the Church of Our Lady of the Rosary form a unit said to be one of the best remaining examples of Federal style architecture. Beneath the belfrey of the church, in a niche, is a 7-foot stone statue of the first American-born saint.

(6:00 a.m. to 5:15 p.m. M-F; 7:30 a.m. to 5:15 p.m. Sat. and Sun.)

85. National Shrine of St. Vincent Ferrer, St. Vincent Ferrer Church, 869 Lexington Avenue

Above the main altar is a triptych honoring the 14th century orator, scholar and miracle worker. In the body of the church, occupying a commanding point of view is a marble statue of the saint. He is depicted wearing the Cappa, the black preaching cloak of the Dominican Order; his hand holds an open book and the flame of the Holy Spirit is above his head. To the right is the Miracle Bell which is rung daily at the services held in his honor. (This commemorates the saintly Dominican's practice of using a bell to call the people of the town together when he was about to preach.) Another custom is the distribution of St. Vincent water.

(6:00 a.m. to 7:00 p.m.)

NEWBURGH

86. Our Lady of Hope Center, 434 River Road

On January 17, 1871 the Blessed Virgin appeared at Pontmain, France. Four children, aged ten to twelve, saw the "Madonna of the Crucifix" in the sky above their village. In the diorama that followed, she revealed her message of "hope through prayer and the cross." A basilica staffed by the Oblates of Mary Immaculate now occupies the site of the apparition. In 1952, the order introduced the devotion to America. At Newburgh they have established a shrine to Our Lady of Hope and conduct novenas in her honor.
(9.00 a.m. to 5:00 p.m.)

NORTH TONAWANDA

87. Infant Jesus Shrine, 3442 Niagra Falls Boulevard

The statue of the Christ Child venerated at this sanctuary is a replica of the one revered at San Salvatore in Onda Church in Rome since the time of St. Vincent Pallotti. Administered by the order he founded, the Society of the Catholic Apostolate, better known as the Pallottine Fathers, the shrine was founded in 1958. Originally housed in a wooden former schoolhouse, a new structure was built and dedicated eleven years later.
(6:30 a.m. to 8:30 p.m.)

PORT EWEN

88. Shrine of Our Lady of the Hudson, Presentation of the Blessed Virgin Church, Minturn Street

On the grounds of the Redemptorist church near the Delaware-Hudson Canal is a six-foot blue stone statue of the Blessed Virgin holding a symbolic tugboat. During the day the tugs salute it with two blasts of their horn and at night they train their search lights on it. Because many boatmen have lost their lives, the families pray to Our Lady of the Hudson for the safety of all those who ply the inland waterways.

ROCHESTER

89. St. Jude's Church, 4100 Lyell Road
Located on the outskirts of the city, the church is noted for its annual novena in honor of the Apostle.
(Always open)

90. Our Lady of Victory Church, 210 Pleasant Street
The Redemptorist Church founded in 1946 is well known throughout the diocese for its Wednesday novenas to Our Lady of Perpetual Help. (There are also weekly devotions to St. Jude, St. Anthony and the saints of the Congregation of the Most Holy Redeemer.) The present church was built in 1890.
(7:00 a.m. to 4:00 p.m. M-F)

SCHODACK LANDING

91. Shrine of St. Jude, Assumption of the Blessed Virgin Mary Church
Devotions to the Saint of the Impossible are held every Monday evening. There is an Annual Solemn Novena nine Mondays prior to the feast day of St. Jude Thaddeus on October 28.
Mailing address: c/o Sacred Heart Church, 22 Stimpson Avenue, Castleton-on-Hudson, NY

TABLEROCK

92. St. Mary's Villa
Staffed by the Sister Servants of Mary Immaculate of the Eastern Catholic Rite, the Villa is three miles west of New York Route 17. The shrine is noted for its lovely Lourdes Grotto and the icon of the Holy Dormition in the chapel. On the weekend prior to the feast of the Assumption there is a pilgrimage, which is especially popular with Ukrainian and Ruthenian Catholics.
Mailing address: Sloatsburg, NY
(10:00 a.m. to 5:00 p.m.)

UTICA

93. St. Mary of Mt. Carmel Church, 648 Jay Street

Served by the priests of the Congregation of the Missionaries of St. Charles, popularly known as the Scalabrinians, the church was founded in 1896 for the spiritual benefit of Italian immigrants. Five years later, Bishop John Baptist Scalabrini of Piacenza, founder of the order, blessed the cornerstone and confirmed 800 children of the parish. The structure was remodeled in 1923, 1936 and 1971. The Utica church is principally known for its annual festival in honor of *Santa Maria di Monte Carmelo* in July. There is also a weekly novena to the church's heavenly patroness.
(7:00 a.m. to 12:00 p.m. M-S; 7:00 a.m. to 1:00 p.m. Sun.)

WATERTOWN

94. Our Lady of the Sacred Heart Church, 666 Thompson Street

When the Missionaries of the Sacred Heart took over St. Mary's they renamed it after their patroness, Our Lady of the Sacred Heart. Though the parish was founded in 1857, the present — the fourth — dates from 1971. The current structure is modern in style and cruciform in plan. The Tabernacle is in the east transept while Our Lady of the Sacred Heart and St. Joseph are honored in the west. The latter two carved wooden statues were designed by Leandro Velasco. The novena to the Sacred Heart Madonna is held each Thursday.

Mailing address: 317 Lynde Street, Watertown, NY
(8:15 a.m. to 4:00 p.m.)

WEST HAVERSTRAW

95. Marian Shrine, Filors Lane

Conducted by the Salesians of Don Bosco, the focal point of the shrine is the 48-foot Rosary Madonna. The six and a half ton bronze statue was cast in Pistoria, Italy in 1959. Blessed by Pope John XXIII, it was first located on the grounds of Good Counsel College in White Plains, New York. Donated to the shrine in 1977, it is mounted on a pedestal of Vermont stone. Among the other features of the Marian sanctuary overlooking the Hudson River are the Rosary Walk, with its sculpture groupings by Henry Arrighini;

Becchi House, a replica of Don Bosco's birthplace; the Altar of Mary, Help of Christians; the Lourdes Grotto; the Fatima Shrine and the Stations of the Cross.
(9:00 a.m. to 5:00 p.m.)

WILLIAMSVILLE

96. Infant Jesus of Praque Shrine, Franciscan Missionary Sisters of the Divine Child, 6380 Main Street

Located on the grounds of the Franciscan Sisters' motherhouse, the shrine was built in 1961. Within the window-walled structure, candles burn 24 hours a day. While many from Western New York and Canada come to pray for their intentions, many others send their offerings and petitions by mail.
(Always open)

YOUNGSTOWN

97. Our Lady of Fatima Shrine, 1023 Swan Road

Located in Niagara County, near Lewiston, the Barnabite Fathers' shrine is not far from the Canadian border. Dedicated in 1956, the Marian sanctuary was built on land donated by Mr. and Mrs. Walter Ciurczak. The most prominent feature of this memorial to Our Lady of Fatima is the church dome covered with two layers of glass and plexiglass depicting the Northern Hemisphere. Rising above this structure is a 13-foot statue of the Blessed Virgin made of Vermont granite. Within we find the famous Peace Mural by Prof. Joseph Slawinski, the main altar of white Carrara marble and the chapels of the Immaculate Heart and of the Blessed Sacrament. The church was elevated to the rank of a basilica in 1975 by Pope Paul VI. Also of interest are the Avenue of Saints, Fatima Hill, the Stations of the Cross, Rosary Pond and Ave Maria Chapel.
(9:00 a.m. to 5:00 p.m. M-S; 9:00 a.m. to 7:00 p.m. Sun.)

PENNSYLVANIA

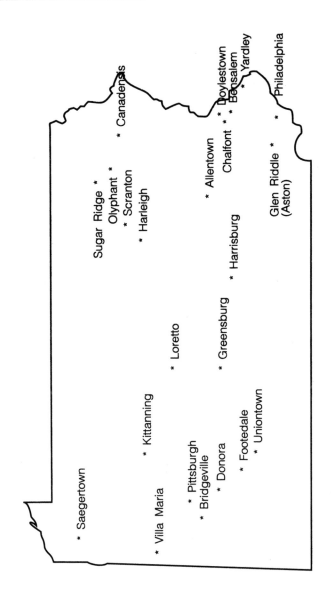

ALLENTOWN

98. National Shrine Center of Our Lady of Guadalupe, Mother of the Americas, Immaculate Conception of the Blessed Virgin Mary Church, 501 Ridge Avenue

More than 400 years ago, the Mother of God appeared to a poor Mexican Indian named Juan Diego and left a portrait of herself miraculously imprinted on his cactus-fiber cloak. Our Lady of Guadalupe is the patroness of Mexico and the Americas. When a special committee of the U.S. Bishops' Conference decided to establish a national sanctuary in her honor, Immaculate Conception Church in Allentown, Pennsylvania was chosen. This historic church was founded in 1857 by St. John Neumann. Dedicated in 1974, the shrine displays an image of Our Lady of Guadalupe said to resemble the original in dimension, color and detail more closely than any other reproduction. There are devotions to the Mexican Madonna each Sunday afternoon.

(Open during services only)

BENSALEM

99. St. Elizabeth Convent, 1663 Bristol Pike

The Mother House of the Sisters of the Blessed Sacrament is the final resting place of Bl. Katherine Drexel, foundress of that order. She is buried in a crypt below the chapel. Many come here to pray for her canonization.

(1:00 p.m. to 5:00 p.m.)

BRIDGEVILLE

100. St. Anthony Church and Shrines, 179 Millers Run Road

The Franciscan church has three shrines, namely those of St. Anthony, Our Lady of Fatima and the Pieta. Probably the most popular is the one dedicated to the Saint from Padua. Though his shrine was not built until 1984, devotions to him began here 35 years before. Novenas to the Franciscan saint are held for thirteen consecutive Tuesdays before the Feast of St. Anthony (June 13th). The Fatima shrine is an outdoor sanctuary constructed in 1956.

Rosary devotions are conducted there during May and October. And, of course, there is an annual May crowning ceremony.
(Always open)

CANADENSIS

101. St. Nicholas Chapel Shrine, Carpathian Village, Snow Hill Road

Off State route 447, in the Pocono Mountains, the Shrine Chapel is the heart of the recreational and renewal center of the Byzantine Catholic Diocese of Passaic. There is an annual pilgrimage.
(By appointment only)

CHALFONT

102. Church of St. Jude, 321 West Butler Avenue

In a chapel set aside as a shrine to the Patron of Difficult Cases stands a beautiful statue of the saint. The church also has a first class relic of St. Jude. Novenas are held each Thursday.
(6:45 a.m. to 7:00 p.m.)

DONORA

103. Holy Name of the Blessed Virgin Mary Church, 320 Second Street

In 1978, Fr. Bernard Kacmarczyk remodeled the church to celebrate the parish's 75th anniversary. Now a beautiful, multi-colored mosaic depicting the last vision of Fatima covers the entry sanctuary. To the left is a Lourdes grotto; on the right is a chapel dedicated to Divine Mercy. Fr. Gino, the noted Italian stigmatist, has predicted a great future for this little church located near Pittsburgh.

DOYLESTOWN

104. National Shrine of Our Lady of Czestochowa, Beacon Hill, Ferry Road

The original icon in Czestochowa, Poland is said to have been painted by St. Luke. Since the 14th century the priests of the Order of St. Paul the Hermit have been guardians of what has become Poland's national shrine. In 1955 the Pauline Fathers established this Marian center, on a 240 acre estate in Bucks County, 25 miles north of Philadelphia. Eleven years later, in order to accommodate an increasing number of pilgrims, a larger and more suitable church was built. The new shrine building was dedicated by Cardinal John Kroll; President Lyndon B. Johnson gave the main address before an audience of 135,000 people. Above the main altar in the upper church hangs a painting of Our Lady of Czestochowa blessed by Pope John XXIII. There is a perpetual novena to the Madonna of Jasna Gora each Sunday (Polish) and Wednesday (English). *(9:00 a.m. to 5:00 p.m.)*

FOOTEDALE

105. St. Maximilian Kolbe Shrine, St. Thomas Church

Dedicated one week after the canonization of the Polish Saint, 1982, the shrine was erected by Fr. Sebastian Pajdzik and the parishioners of St. Thomas Church. The sanctuary resembles a prison cell in the concentration camp at Auschwitz where St. Maximilian Kolbe died after voluntarily taking the place of another prisoner in the starvation bunker. Above the entrance of the outdoor shrine are the words "the path of freedom is marked by the cross." Inside there is a marble altar and a sculpture by Adam Fuks depicting the Blessed Virgin appearing to the Franciscan Conventual Saint in a vision.

Mailing address: New Salem, PA
(Always open)

GLEN RIDDLE

106. St. John Neumann Shrine, Our Lady of Angels Convent (Aston)

On the grounds of the motherhouse of the Sisters of St. Francis, an order co-founded by St. John Neumann, is a shrine sheltering the altar at which the saintly Bishop of Philidelphia accepted the vows of the first members of the community on May 26, 1856.

Mailing address: Aston, PA
(Daylight hours)

GREENSBURG

107. St. Walburga Shrine, St. Emma Convent and Retreat House, 1001 Harvey Street

Born in England in 710, St. Walburga was the sister of Saints Willibald and Winebald. After becoming a Benedictine nun, she accompanied St. Lioba to Germany where the two assisted St. Boniface in bringing Christianity to the pagan Germans. She was later appointed abbess of a monastery at Heidenheim. Her remains are at Eichstatt, Bavaria; the oil secreted by her bones is said to have curative powers. Her American shrine, dedicated in 1974, is a star-shaped chapel on the grounds of the Benedictine Sisters' motherhouse in Greensburg. The walls of this structure were originally twelve stained glass windows from St. Walburga Church in Pittsburgh.
(Daylight hours)

HARLEIGH

108. Sacred Heart Shrine, 1 Church Place

Dedicated in 1975, this is the largest outdoor sanctuary consecrated to this popular Catholic devotion. The shrine's five plateaus are linked by a multi-colored geometric walk along which are plaques depicting the Twelve Promises to St. Margaret Mary Alacoque. The focal point is the main altar above which rises the statue to the Sacred Heart, made of Carrara marble. To the left of the main plaza is the Way of the Cross culminating in a crucifixion scene, tomb of Christ and a statue of Our Risen Savior.
(Always open)

HARRISBURG

109. Shrine of the Miraculous Medal, St. Catherine Laboure Church, 4000 Derry Street

Founded one year after her canonization, this was the first parish in the world to be dedicated to St. Catherine Laboure. Twenty-eight years later, in 1976 the Shrine of the Miraculous Medal was erected under the guidance of Msgr. Leo A. Beierschmitt. The circular chapel is noted for its stained glass windows designed by Gabriel

Loire of Chartes, France. There are weekly devotions in honor of Our Lady of the Miraculous Medal.
(6:45 a.m. to 8:00 p.m.)

KITTANNING

110. Shrine of Our Lady of Guadalupe, St. Mary Church, 101 West High Street

The present church, begun by Fr. Francis X. Foley was completed in 1964 by his successor as pastor, Msgr. Charles B. Guth. Approaching the church, one first encounters, in the front plaza, the 10-foot bronze statue of Mary, the Mother of God. Dominating the interior is the Minnesota granite altar above which towers the 20-foot crucifix made from the main beam of the original St. Mary's Church built in 1853. The corpus and the wooden statues in the church were carved by Edmund Rabanser of Ortisei, Italy. The chapel, to the right of the altar, is both the Blessed Sacrament Chapel and the Diocesan Shrine of Our Lady of Guadalupe. Above the tabernacle on the altar of reserve is a mosaic telling the story of Our Lady of Guadalupe. Covering an area of 504 square feet, it was designed by Duncan Niles Terry. The windows of the chapel trace the history of the Catholic Church in this area.
(7:00 a.m. to 7:00 p.m.)

LORETTO

Formerly known as McGuire's Settlement, the town's name was changed to Loretto by Prince Gallitzin, a Russian emigre priest who labored here 1799-1840. Scattered throughout this mountain community are a number of historic and religious shrines, the largest such collection in the country. During the summer months Loretto is a mecca for tourists and retreatants. The various shrines are listed in the traditional manner, following the route which pilgrims customarily take.

111. Prince Gallitzin Chapel House

Born in the Hague, Holland in 1770, Demetrius Gallitzin was the son of the Russian ambassador. Raised as an athiest, the prince was introduced to the faith at age 17 by his mother who had recently

undergone a conversion. Five years later he announced his decision to become a priest to the astonishment of his parents. Journeying to the United States, he was ordained by Bishop Carroll of Baltimore in 1795. (It is interesting to note that Carroll was the first U.S. bishop and Gallitzin was the second priest to be ordained in America.) After serving at Conewego, Pennsylvania, the priest-prince was assigned to McGuire's Settlement in 1799. He decided to build a model Christian community here; using his own money he built a church, tannery, sawmill and gristmill. To encourage people to settle in Loretto, he bought land, lumber and cattle and established storehouses for food, medical supplies, tools, farm implements and other basic necessities. The saintly priest was so dedicated to the people of western Pennsylvania that he refused the bishoprics of Philadelphia, Louisville, Cincinnati and Detroit when they were offered to him. In 1832 he built the Chapel House which was to serve as his residence and private chapel. Here the "Apostle of the Alleghenies" died eight years later. The building is open to the public. Visitors may view his chalice, Mass Book, relic of the True Cross and other mementos.
(Daylight hours)

112. Our Lady of the Alleghenies Shrine

Designed by Sister Mary Benedicta San Antonio, the statuary group depicts the Blessed Mother in pioneer garb, her hands outstreched in benediction, smiling compassionately at a mountain child as a small deer looks on. Dedicated in September 1951, Our Lady of the Alleghenies is the official Marian shrine of the diocese of Altoona and the object of an annual pilgrimage on August 22, the Feast of the Immaculate Heart of Mary.
(Always open)

113. Father Gallitzin's Tomb

After his death in 1840, the pastor of Loretto was, according to his last request, buried just outside the entrance to his church. In 1899, on the centenary of his arrival, a bronze likeness of the "Apostle of the Alleghenies" was erected over his crypt.

114. St. Michael Church

The present structure built in 1899 is a gift of Charles M. Schwab, founder of Bethlehem Steel Corporation. The basilica-like building has a seating capacity of 900 in the church proper and an additional 200 in the gallery. The first church on this site was built by Father Gallitzin, completed in time for the Christmas midnight Mass a century before. The original church was replaced in 1817 and again in 1854.

(7:00 a.m. to 4:00 p.m.)

115. Grotto of Our Lady of Lourdes

Built to commemorate the apparitions of the Blessed Virgin to St. Bernadette Soubirous in 1858, the grotto is a replica of that at Lourdes, France. The shrine was constructed by Fr. Charles Ginocchio on the site of the quarry from which stones were taken for the original buildings at St. Frances College in 1847. The grotto was blessed in 1937.

116. Immaculate Conception Chapel

The chapel of St. Francis College replaces the one destroyed in the great fire of 1942. The school is under the direction of the Franciscan Fathers of the Third Order Regular (T. O. R.).

117. Our Lady of Fatima Shrine

While gravely ill and in danger of loosing his life, Fr. Bernard Cuskelly promised that if he recovered he would build a sanctuary to the Immaculata. In fulfillment of his vow, the Fatima Shrine was erected in October 1951 — the most recently built of the Loretto pilgrimage stations. Located on the grounds of Mt. Assisi Monastery, it memorializes the appearance of the Blessed Virgin to three shepherd children in Portugal early in this century. Devotions to Our Lady of Fatima are held here on the 13th of each month from May to October.

118. Carmelite Monastery

Founded in 1930 by a community of Discalced Carmelite Nuns

from France, the chapel dedicated to the Little Flower is open to the public. Groups visiting Loretto on Sunday often conclude their pilgrimage with 4:00 p.m. Benediction of the Blessed Sacrament at the Sisters' Oratory. There is also a well attended annual Solemn Novena in honor of Our Lady of Mt. Carmel and St. Therese of Lisieux prior to October 1.
(9:00 a.m. to 5:00 p.m.)

OLYPHANT

119. *Shrine of Our Lady of Zhrovytsi, SS. Cyril and Methodius Church, 135 River Street*

More than 900 years ago in northeastern Ukraine, shepherd children saw a mysterious light on a wild pear tree. Investigating they found an icon of the Blessed Mother. A church was soon built to house it. Later, in 1613, the shrine was placed in the care of the Basilian Fathers whose founder, St. Josaphat, was devoted to Our Lady of Zhrovytsi. A hundred years later, a copy of the icon was discovered in Rome and is now enshrined in the Church of Madonna dei Monti. In 1980, the Olyphant shrine was dedicated at the hundred-year-old Ukranian Catholic Church. Since 1983, there has been an annual pilgrimage.

PHILADELPHIA

120. *National Shrine of St. John Neumann, St. Peter the Apostle Church, 1019 North 5th Street*

Born at Prachatiz, Bohemia in the early Nineteenth Century, St. John Neumann was the fourth bishop of Philadelphia and the first American male to be canonized. Ordained in 1836 in New York, he entered the Redemptorists four years later and became the first of that order to take his vows in the United States. Within five years, he became vice-regent of the Congregation of the Most Holy Redeemer. In 1852, against his will, he was consecrated Bishop of Philadelphia. During the next eight years, he established eighty churches; brought seven religious orders into his diocese; co-founded the Sisters of St. Francis of Glen Riddle; authored two widely used catechisms and put into operation a central administration for his parochial schools. He died

in 1860 at age forty-nine. In compliance with his request, he was buried in the basement chapel of St. Peter's Redemptorist Church. Thousands have visited his tomb, attended the daily novenas and viewed the artifacts in the St. John Neumann Museum.
(7:30 a.m. to 6:00 p.m.)

121. Shrine of Blessed Margaret of Castello, Holy Name of Jesus Church, 701 East Gaul Street

Born blind, crippled, hunchbacked and a dwarf, the 13th century Italian is the patroness of the unwanted. Her parents were so disgusted by her appearance that they shut her up in a cell adjoining a church in the forest. At age 13, they took her to Citti di Castello in the hope that she would be cured at the tomb of Fra Giacomo. The strategy failed, so her parents abandoned her. She then entered a convent but was expelled shortly after. Finally she became a Dominican tertiary. She won over many through her piety, patient endurance and charity. Her body now lies beneath the high altar at the Church of St. Domenico at Citti di Castello; after 650 years it is still incorrupt. At the Philadelphia Dominican Church there is a perpetual novena in honor of Bl. Margaret of Castello every morning of the week. In addition, three solemn novenas are conducted each year.
(7:45 a.m. to 9:00 p.m.)

122. Mary's Central Shrine of the Miraculous Medal, Immaculate Conception Chapel, St. Vincent's Seminary, 500 East Chelten Avenue

One of the most popular Catholic sacramentals is the Miraculous Medal. Its design was revealed to St. Catherine Laboure by the Blessed Virgin during a series of visions in Paris during the first half of the 19th century. In 1915, Fr. Joseph A. Skelly, a Vincentian priest, founded the Central Association of the Miraculous Medal to promote devotion to Mary Immaculate. Over the years, the organization has distributed more than 75 million medals and almost 40 million booklets telling the story of this sacramental. In 1927, Mary's Central Shrine was built. Crowning the lofty tower of the chapel of St. Vincent's Seminary is a heroic statue of the Blessed Virgin. The interior of the shrine is furnished in marble and golden

Venetian-style mosaics. Above the tabernacle of the main altar stands a magnificent statue of Our Lady, hands out-stretched in the pose memorialized on the Miraculous Medal. Another smaller shrine is located in the lower church. Here Mary is depicted as she appeared at the start of the second apparition to St. Catherine at the Rue du Bac Chapel in 1830. Nine novena services in honor of Our Lady of the Miraculous Medal are conducted each Monday. *(11:00 a.m. to 4:00 p.m.)*

123. *Shrine of Our Lady of Knock, St. Richard's Church, 3010 South 18th Street*

On August 21, 1879 at Knock in County Mayo, Ireland, fifteen people, aged six to seventy-five witnessed a vision. The figures of Mary, Joseph and St. John the Evangelist appeared against the wall of the south gable of the village church. To the right was an altar surmounted by a lamb beneath a cross. The shrine at Knock is now Ireland's most famous Marian sanctuary. Built by Fr. John J. Morley, the Philadelphia center for the veneration of the Gaelic Madonna has a large painting of the apparition, a statue and a small oratory in the rear of the church called the Chapel of Saints and Apparitions. Novena devotions are held every Tuesday evening from September through May.
(Daylight hours; use side door)

124. *Grotto of Our Lady of Lourdes, Provincial Motherhouse of the Sisters of St. Basil the Great, 710 Fox Chase Road*

The first pilgrimage to the Ukranian Catholic shrine located on the grounds of the motherhouse took place on Mother's Day 1938. Each year there is another.

125. *Our Lady of Victories Shrine, St. Peter Claver Church, 502 South 12th Street*

Administered by the Holy Ghost Fathers, the church was founded by Fr. Patrick McDermott in 1889 to serve as a mission to Philadelphia's Black population. As the parish grew a new church, formerly Presbyterian, was purchased. In 1898, the shrine of Our Lady of Victory was erected at St. Peter Claver Church by

Archbishop Patrick J. Ryan of Philadelphia. Its Confraternity of the Most Holy and Immaculate Heart of Mary is affiliated with the Archconfraternity in Paris. A perpetual novena to Our Lady of Victory is conducted every Thursday evening.
(Open during services only)

126. St. Rita of Cascia Church, 1166 South Broad Street

Born to elderly parents in late 14th century Italy, St. Rita was a devout child. Married at age twelve, perhaps against her will, she endured eighteen unhappy years with her boorish husband. After his death, and that of her two sons, she tried unsuccessfully to enter a convent of Augustinian nuns. On her third try she was finally accepted. She distinguished herself by her piety, austerities and concern for others. St. Rita experienced visions and bore a wound on her forehead from the crown of thorns. She was canonized in 1900. The South Philadelphia church administered by the Augustinians has been a center of veneration of the Saint from Umbria for many decades. In 1922, Pope Pius XI granted a Plenary Indulgence to all those attending the Annual Solemn Novena, May 14 to May 22 at St. Rita of Cascia Church. There is also a perpetual novena each Wednesday morning. The church also distributes St. Rita Oil and Rose Petals.
(Open during services only)

PITTSBURGH

127. Blessed Nunzio Sulprizo Shrine, 1138 Stanford Road

Born in Italy in 1817, Bl. Nunzio's life was one of suffering patiently endured. His father died soon after his birth. After his mother remarried, his step father mistreated him. Then she died and the child was sent to live with his maternal grandmother. But the kindly woman had only a short time to live. Three years later he came under the care of his uncle Domenico Luciano who treated him even worse than his stepfather had. From him he received constant scoldings, threats and physical abuse. He never had sufficient food or clothing. Eventually he was rescued by another uncle, Francesco Sulprizo who took him to live with him in Naples. But soon he was in the hospital suffering from convulsions and later dropsy. He died

in 1836, at the age of only nineteen. He is the patron of laborers and abused children. On his feast day, May 2, bus loads of people from the East and Midwest come to St. Cyril of Alexandria Church nearby to pray for his canonization.
(10:00 a.m. to 9:00 p.m.)

128. St. Anthony Chapel, 1704 Harpster Street, Troy Hill

Situated on Troy Hill overlooking the Allegheny River, the shrine dedicated to the Wonder Worker of Padua has been designated a historical landmark by the Pittsburgh History and Landmarks Foundation. Enshrined in this unique chapel are more than 5,000 relics collected by Fr. Anthony Mollinger over a period of forty years. Dedicated in 1883, the oratory was expanded nine years later and after falling into disrepair, was restored in 1977. Among the chapel's prized possessions are a first class relic of St. Anthony of Padua and a reliquary in the shape of the cross holding a thorn from the Crown of Thorns, a splinter of the True Cross and a piece of stone from the Holy Sepulchre. Beneath the main altar is the body of St. Demetrius and behind the tabernacle are relics of the saints whose names were formerly mentioned in the Canon of the Mass (The altar itself is said to contain a fragment of the table of the Last Supper.) The shrine also has 17 beautiful stained glass windows and life-sized antique wooden Stations of the Cross. The chapel is closed on Mondays, Wednesdays and Fridays.
(1:00 p.m. to 4:00 p.m. Tues., Thur., Sat.; 11:00 a.m. to 4:00 p.m. Sun.)

SAEGERTOWN

129. Roadside Shrine of Our Lady (U.S. Rt. 19)

Two miles south of town stands the statue of the Blessed Virgin erected during World War II. Maintained by the Catholic Federation of Area Parishes, devotions are held there twice yearly — once during May and in August near the Feast of the Assumption. Mailing address: c/o St. Bernadette Church, Sagerstown, Pennsylvania.

SCRANTON

130. St. Ann's Monastery National Shrine, 1230 St. Ann Street

At the invitation of Bishop M.J. Hoban, the Passionists established a monastery in Scranton in 1905. In the same year, they began the practice of holding a novena to their patron, St. Ann. At first the services were private, limited to members of the Congregation of the Passion. But in 1924 the public was invited. The response was overwhelming. Soon the small chapel in the monastery proved unable to hold the large number of pilgrims. A tent was then erected, followed by a temporary wooden structure. In 1929, the Lombardy Renaissance monastery church was dedicated. Here weekly novenas to St. Ann are held four times a day each Monday. Large crowds, numbering in the thousands, attend the annual Solemn Novena July 17 to 26th.

(9:00 a.m. to 8:00 p.m. M-F; 9:00 a.m. to 5:00 p.m. Sat. and Sun.)

SUGAR RIDGE

131. St. John Neumann Shrine, SS. Philip and James Church

In 1852, while visiting Overton, Bishop Neumann became aware that there were more Catholics in a nearby town. Journeying there he said Mass for the people of Sugar Ridge and encouraged them to build a chapel. Two years later, he returned to bless the log church and administer Confirmation. He did the same in 1856 and 1858. Later the old church was replaced with a larger building. Over the years most of the residents have moved away from this town in the section of the Alleghenies called the Endless Mountains. But in 1966, the deserted wooden church was declared a shrine by Bishop J. Carroll McCormick of Scranton. Now large numbers of pilgrims attend the three annual Masses held there during the summer months.

Mailing address: c/o Church of St. Basil, Dushore, PA

(Open during services only)

UNIONTOWN

132. Our Lady of Perpetual Help Shrine, Mount St. Macrina Retreat Center, 510 West Main Street

Mount St. Macrina with its over 100 acres of natural beauty dotted with outdoor shrines and chapels faces U.S. Route 40 near Uniontown in the foothills of the Laurel Mountains. Operated by the Byzantine Rite Sisters of St. Basil since 1935, the Marian sanctuary has been the focal point of an annual pilgrimage of thousands of Eastern and Latin Rite Catholics. In recent years, the average attendance was between twenty-five and thirty thousand, making it one of the most popular Marian shrines in America. Perhaps as many as two million visitors came here over the years. The object of pilgrimage is a beautiful icon of Our Lady of Perpetual Help given to the Mt. Saint Macrina sisters by Pope Pius XI. The principal liturgies are celebrated by one or more bishops. The famous televangelist Archbishop Fulton J. Sheen preached homilies here on more than one occasion.
(9:00 a.m. to 4:00 p.m.)

VILLA MARIA

133. Villa Maria Community Center

Located on the western border of Pennsylvania, a few miles from Youngstown, Ohio, the grounds of the mother-house of the Sisters of the Humility of Mary contain two shrines. The first honors Our Lady of Lourdes and was given to the sisters by Leopold Rohrer in 1896. It is not a grotto but rather a rounded structure of great sandstone blocks in an archaic style. The sanctuary was renovated and rededicated in 1979. The other shrine is dedicated to Our Lady of the Villa. Its focal point is a statue of the Blessed Virgin brought from France in 1864 by the first sisters of this community to come to this country. It is said of the one-armed image of the Mother holding her Child, that on one occasion in its native country, Our Lady of the Villa came alive and made a courteous bow to Mother Magdelen, foundress of the order. The statue is enclosed in a small chapel moved to its present location in 1955.

YARDLEY

134. Bl. Marguerite D'Youville Shrine, Sacred Heart Chapel, Grey Nuns of the Sacred Heart Motherhouse, Quarry Road

Dedicated in 1966, the shrine is located in the foyer of the sisters' chapel. Since 1982 there has been a weekly novena for the canonization of Bl. Marguerite D'Youville, the foundress of the Grey Nuns.

(Open on request)

RHODE ISLAND

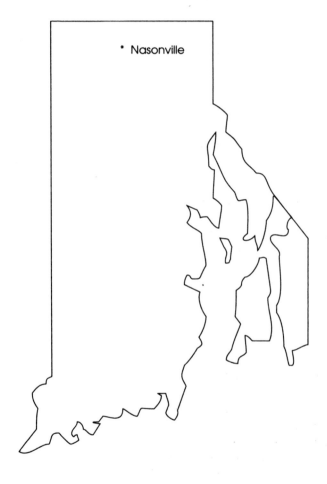

* Nasonville

NASONVILLE

135. Shrine of the Little Flower, St. Theresa's Church, 7 Dion Drive

This chapel on the grounds of the Nasonville parish church is the oldest shrine dedicated to the "Saint of the Little Way" in America. The outdoor sanctuary is constructed of ornamental stone and brick, replacing the wooden one created in 1927-1928 by Fr. Alphonse P. Desroachers. The original impetus for the popularity of the shrine came from the miraculous recovery of Mrs. Olivier Faford, a parishioner, through the intercession of St. Therese of Lisieux. Also in the grove are the fourteen Stations of the Cross created by Amedeo Nardini and the Sancta Scala. The Holy Stairs are made of fieldstone, limestone and granite and are patterned after those Jesus ascended and descended during his Passion. Pious pilgrims mount the twenty-eight steps on their knees.
(Daylight hours)

VERMONT

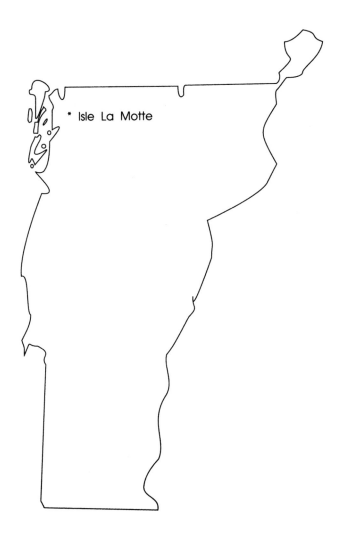

* Isle La Motte

ISLE LA MOTTE

136. St. Anne's Shrine

Situated on an island in Lake Champlain, the shrine is conducted by the Edmundite Fathers and Brothers. It is here that the great French explorer Samuel de Champlain landed in 1609. A majestic granite statue marks the spot. Isle la Motte was the site of Fort St. Anne, constructed in 1666, where the first Mass in Vermont was celebrated. Each year, in July, the traditional Triduum of St. Anne is held, consisting of an evening liturgy followed by a candlelight procession. Other attractions are the Marian grotto, the Way of the Cross and the little outdoor shrine to St. Anne. Because of weather conditions, the shrine is only open May 15 to October 15. *(Daylight hours)*

PART TWO:
SHRINES OF THE MIDWEST

Illinois
Indiana
Iowa
Kansas
Michigan
Minnesota
Nebraska
North Dakota
Ohio
South Dakota
Wisconsin

ILLINOIS

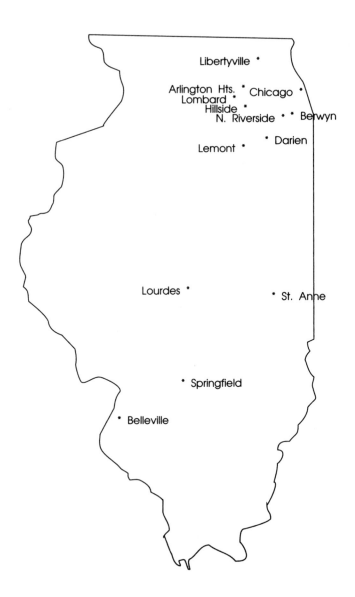

ARLINGTON HEIGHTS

137. Our Lady of the Wayside Church, 432 West Park Street

In the City of Rome the famous Gesu Church boasts a 5th century fresco known as Our Lady of the Way. A favorite of St. Ignatius Loyola, St. Francis de Sales and many other saints, the image received papal crowns in 1638 and 1865. As the fame of the Gesu Madonna spread, shrines in her honor arose in Germany, Ireland, Scotland and England. The Arlington Heights church houses a replica of the Madonna della Strada made in 1953 by a distinguished Italian artist. Novenas to Our Lady of the Wayside are held every Tuesday.

(6:00 a.m. until dusk)

BELLEVILLE

138. National Shrine of Our Lady of Snows, 9500 west Illinois Route 5

According to legend, devotion to Our Lady under this title began sixteen centuries ago in the city of Rome. It is said that on the night of August 4, 352, the Blessed Virgin appeared to Pope Liberius and the Patrician John and his wife in a dream. Our Lady asked that a church be built in her honor at a place which she would indicate. When the people of the Eternal City awoke the following morning, they found the Esquiline Hill covered with snow. Today the Basilica of St. Mary Major stands on the same hill. Many centuries later, St. Henry's Seminary in Belleville, Illinois became a center of devotion to Our Lady of Snows. Novenas to her became so popular that in 1958, the Oblate Fathers began building what was to become one of the most popular pilgrimage destinations in the country. The 200-acre shrine has a huge modernistic outdoor altar, a 6,200 seat amphitheater and an indoor chapel. Also among its attractions are the Relic Chapel containing 1,500 relics and the Rosary Court consisting of altars honoring each of the joyful, sorrowful or glorious mysteries. Not to be overlooked are the outdoor Way of the Cross, the Lourdes Grotto and the Annunciation Garden.

(8:00 a.m. to 8:00 p.m.)

BERWYN

139. National Shrine of the Poor Souls, St. Odilo Church, 2244 South East Avenue

It was St. Odilo, the 10th century Benedictine Abbot of Cluny, France, who inaugurated the custom of commemorating the deceased members of his monastery the day after the feast of All Souls. The influence of Cluny was so great that the practice spread throughout Europe. This is the origin of All Souls' Day. It was Cardinal George Mundelein of Chicago who commissioned the building of this church in 1927 and who officially declared it to be the National Shrine of the Souls in Purgatory. Every Wednesday there is a Novena for the Poor Souls.
(6:30 a.m. to 5:30 p.m.)

CHICAGO

140. National Shrine of St. Anne, St. Joseph and St. Anne Church, 2751 West 38th Place

This red brick gothic structure, originally called St. Joseph Church, was established to serve the needs of French Canadians living in the Brighton Park district of Chicago's south side. Knowing his parishioners' devotion to the grandmother of Jesus, Father Cyril A. Poissant erected a St. Anne shrine at the church in 1900. Thus began the famous annual novena to St. Anne de Brighton with its candle light processions and guest speakers. The shrine chapel features a statue similar to that at St. Anne de Beaupre in Canada.
(Open during services only)

141. Franciscan Shrines of St. Francis and St. Anthony, St. Peter's Church, 110 West Madison

On the night of October 9, 1871 during the Great Chicago Fire, parishioners of this Franciscan church promised a perpetual shrine and devotion to St. Anthony of Padua if they were spared. Early the following morning, the flames changed direction barely two blocks from the church. Located in Chicago's famous Loop, St. Peter's frequent weekday Masses, St. Anthony Novenas and first Saturday devotions draw many downtown shoppers and office workers, as well as out-of-town visitors. Though the parish was established in

1844, the current edifice dates to 1954. The outside facade is dominated by "the Christ of the Loop" an 18 foot, 26 ton statue of our crucified Savior. The interior walls are of pink marble adorned by 10 white base-relief panels depicting the life of St. Francis. To the left and right of the sanctuary are shrines to St. Anthony of Padua and the Poverello respectively.
(6:00 a.m. to 7:00 p.m.)

142. Holy Rosary Church, 612 North Western Avenue
Established at the turn of the century, the parish is noted for its devotion to St. Roch. Each year there is a novena prior to his feast. On the Sunday closest to the Saint's Day, a major celebration is held complete with Mass and a procession featuring a nearly life-size statue of St. Roch.
(Open during services only)

143. Holy Trinity Croatian Catholic, 1850 South Throop Street
Built in 1915, this Dominican staffed church was established to serve Catholics of Croatian descent. Because of the devotion which his South Slavic parishioners had for Our Lady of Bistrica, Father Innocent M. Bojanic established a shrine to her in 1938. After Vatican II, the church was renovated and the shrine given a modern look. Each year in August the feast of Our Lady of Bistrica is celebrated. The liturgy is in Croatian, of course. Girls in colorful native costume carrying the image of Our Lady accompany the procession through the streets of the parish.
(Open during services only)

144. St. John of God Church, 1634 West 52nd Street
Overlooking Sherman Park, this Renaissance-style church was built in 1920. Though at one time the church served as many as 2,400 families, the economic decline of the area and the influx of non-Catholics has resulted in reduced enrollment. Devotion to St. Mary, the Mystical Rose has however, helped to renew the parish. (Veneration to Our Lady under this title has its origin in a series of apparitions in the diocese of Brescia in Northern Italy). The imported linden wood statue of Maria Mystica Rosa at St. John of God Church was seen to shed tears four times during the latter part of May 1984.
(6:30 a.m. to 5:30 p.m. Mon., Wed., Fri.; 6:30 a.m. to 8:30 p.m. Tue., Thur.; 6:30 a.m. to 6:30 p.m. Sat. and Sun.)

145. National Shrine of St. Jude, Our Lady of Guadalupe Church, 3208 East 91st Street

Construction of the Claretian staffed church began in 1928. However, the following year with the onset of the Depression, the steel mills began laying off many parishioners and it seemed that Our Lady of Guadalupe Church would not be completed. But Fr. James T. Tort did not despair. Instead, he promised St. Jude, a then largely unknown saint, that he would erect a shrine to him if enough money could be raised to finish the church. That year novenas to the patron saint of difficult or impossible cases began. Little by little the money came in, construction was completed and a modest shrine installed. As the Great Depression deepened, more and more visitors began to frequent the church and devotion to St. Jude began to spread throughout the country. Today five Solemn Novenas are held each year.
(7:00 a.m. to 8:00 p.m. M-S; 7:00 a.m. to 7:00 p.m. Sun.)

146. Shrine of St. Jude Thaddeus, St. Pius V Church, 1909 South Ashland Avenue

There are two centers of devotion to St. Jude in Chicago. The Dominican administered church which houses the other shrine was constructed in 1893. The shrine itself was established in 1929. (Surprisingly, both shrines came into existence in the same year). The attractive interior of St. Pius V Church features a statuary group honoring St.Jude. And directly opposite is an area devoted to Our Lady of Guadalupe, a favorite of the Mexican-American parishioners. Devotions to St. Jude are held weekly, and several times a year there are Solemn Novenas to the Saint of the Impossible.
(7:00 a.m. to 6:30 p.m. Mon.-Wed., Fri.; 7:00 a.m. to 7:30 p.m. Thur.; 7:00 a.m. to 8:45 p.m. Sat.; 7:00 a.m. to 6:00 p.m. Sun.)

147. Mother Cabrini Shrine, Columbus Hospital, 2520 North Lake Shore Drive

Frances Xavier Cabrini, founder of the Missionary Sisters of the Sacred Heart and the first American to be canonized, came to this country in 1889. Much of her time in the United States was spent in Chicago, where she built three hospitals. Mother Cabrini's room at Columbus Hospital has been preserved, for it is here that she died in

1917. Entrance to this chamber is via a commerative chapel fitted with a high octagonal dome and ornamented in bronze and marble. Ceiling murals tell the life of the saint and a side altar features a statue showing her praying to the Sacred Heart of Jesus. *(8:00 a.m. to 5:00 p.m.)*

148. St. Michael Church, 1633 North Cleveland Avenue

When the Redemptorist Fathers and Brothers were entrusted with the original picture at St. Alphonsus Church in Rome, Pope Pius IX told them "make Our Mother of Perpetual Help known throughout the world." Since that time, the order has dedicated itself to this task. So, it should come as no surprise that when the Congregation of the Most Holy Redeemer was given direction of this church in 1860, they began the propagation of this devotion. In 1904, the ornate Shrine of our Mother of Perpetual Help, which still serves as the focal point for the church's two novenas every Tuesday, was erected. Each year there is a popular Triduum in honor of Our Lady. The Redemptorists also staff St. Alphonsus Church (1429 West Wellington), which has devotions to Our Lady of Perpetual Help three times a day on Tuesdays.
(Open during services only)

149. Nativity of the Blessed Virgin Mary Church, 6812 South Western Avenue

In 1608, the Mother of God appeared to a group of children near Siluva, Lithuania. When immigrants from the Baltic country came to the Marquette Park area of Chicago, they brought with them a devotion to this Madonna. Named after the Old Country shrine, the church has become a center of devotion to Our Lady of Siluva. Though the parish was founded in 1927, the present church, whose architecture mingles Baroque style with Lithuanian folk art, was dedicated in 1957. Dominating the main altar is a hammered brass and gold portrait of the church's patroness. Each year there is a popular novena in her honor ending on September 8th, the feast day of Our Lady of Siluva.
(Open during services only)

150. National Shrine of Our Sorrowful Mother, Our Lady of Sorrows Basilica, 3121 West Jackson Boulevard

Although this Servite-administered parish on Chicago's west side was established in 1874, the present church was not completed until 28 years later. In January, 1937, Fr. James Keane inaugurated a perpetual novena to Our Sorrowful Mother. It was an overnight success. A year later, attendance had grown to 70,000 for the thirty-eight novena services held each Friday. Soon devotion to Our Lady of Sorrows spread to other parishes in the city, then to other states and eventually around the world. The twenty years following 1937 were this shrine's "glory years." Among the activities during this period were the publication of *Novena Notes*, a magazine which at one time had almost one million readers. And the church was the site of the filming of "The Eternal Gift," a full length movie about Solemn High Mass. In 1956, Pope Pius XII designated Our Lady of Sorrows as a basilica. But then a steep decline began. Due to the change in the racial makeup of the parish, the advent of television and the liturgical changes accompanying Vatican II, the novenas have almost disappeared. But the 1980s have brought a renewal. First Saturday and other special services are drawing people back to the newly redecorated church. Among the sights that await visitors to the church are the Pieta Chapel containing a replica of Michelangelo's famous sculpture done by Ferdinand Pella. To the right and left of the sanctuary are the shrine altars of Our Sorrowful Mother and the Seven Holy Founders of the Servite Order. Along the wall are the stations of the Via Matris commemorating the Blessed Virgin's seven sorrows.
(7:00 a.m. to 4:00 p.m. M-Sun.)

151. National Shrine of St. Peregrine, St. Dominic's Church, 357 West Locust Street

The "Cancer Saint" was born in 1265 in Forli, Italy. Though at one time a fervent anti-papist, under the influence of St. Philip Benizi, he reformed and eventually joined the Servite order. St. Peregrine Laziosi was known for his austerities and for his preaching. Much of his fame is due to his miraculous recovery from cancer after experiencing a vision. The national shrine to this saint is

located in St. Dominic's, a twin towered, red brick Gothic church in the midst of one of Chicago's poorest, most crime-ridden, black housing project areas.
(Open during services only)

152. Queen of All Saints Basilica, 6280 North Sauganash Avenue
Begun in 1956 and consecrated four years later, this huge edifice was elevated to the rank of a Basilica shortly after its consecration. Above the cathedral-like structure is a copper spire, supported by a single tower. Inside, the "Window of the Apparitions" over the choir loft commemorates nine of St. Mary's most famous appearances. Serving as a centerpiece for the main altar is a reredos of the Queen of All Saints. Novenas in her honor are held every Wednesday.
(6:30 a.m. until dark)

153. Sacred Heart Shrine, Felician Sisters Provincial House Chapel, 3800 West Peterson Avenue
While visiting a statuary company, Sister Mary Angelina became enthralled by a statue of the Sacred Heart of Jesus. With money donated by a generous elderly woman, she purchased it for her school several months later. For the next seven years, the image reigned over Good Counsel High School from its place in a bend in the fourth floor corridor. Here the Sacred Heart drew to himself numerous devotees and many favors were granted. As the statue's fame grew, at the request of Cardinal George Mundelein, it was transferred on March 4, 1936, to its present location in the sister's provincial house chapel. With proper ecclesiastic approval, a Novena of Confidence to the Sacred Heart was printed and circulated. In the first year, 27,000 requests for the novena poured in. They came from all over the country — and from Europe and Asia as well. The chapel remains open to the public; the Blessed Sacrament is exposed daily. Also on the grounds is a Lourdes grotto.
(7:00 a.m. to 4:00 p.m.)

154. St. Rita Church, 6243 South Fairfield Avenue
Built in 1949 and dedicated on Thanksgiving Day 1950, this stately Romanesque structure is large enough to be a cathedral or basilica. Since the parish was founded, the Augustinian Fathers have

held an annual novena to St. Rita of Cascia. (St. Rita shares with St. Jude the honor of being considered the Saint of the Impossible.) The novena begins on May 13 and closes on May 22. The following day, the Feast of St. Rita is celebrated with a special Liturgy.
(Open during services only)

DARIEN

155. St. Therese Aylesford Chapel and Museum, Carmelite Visitors Center, Cass Avenue at I-55

When the Carmelites were driven from the Holy Land by the Saracens, a new home was found at Aylesford Manor in England. It was here that St. Simon Stock is believed to have received the scapular from the Blessed Virgin more than 700 years ago. So when Father Francis Rafferty and Father Alexis McCarthy began building this place in 1959, they named it Aylesford. Also called the Carmelite Visitors Center, it consists of a shrine-chapel dedicated to the Little Flower, a museum and a large religious gift and book store. Among the highlights of the devotional chapel are a large wooden base-relief picturing the Little Flower and ten scenes from her life. The shrine has five major relics of the saint.
(10:00 a.m. to 4:00 p.m.; closed holidays)

HILLSIDE

156. Our Lady of Lebanon Church, 425 North Hillside

Born in 1828 in the village of Biqa-Kafra, Lebanon, St. Sharbel entered monastic life at the age of 23. Most of the following forty-seven years were spent in or near St. Maron Monastery, first as a monk then as a hermit. Several months after his death, a bright light was seen surrounding his tomb. When it was opened, his body was found to show no sign of decay. Since that time, a bloodlike fluid with miraculous healing properties has flowed from the saint's corpse. Our Lady of Lebanon Church was founded in 1953 on Chicago's west side and moved to Hillside twenty years later. Since 1982 devotions to St. Sharbel and the Maronite Madonna are held each Tuesday at this Eastern-rite church on the site of what was once Mater Dolorosa Seminary.
(Open during services only)

LEMONT

157. Tomb of Mother Mary Theresa Dudzik, Franciscan Sisters' Motherhouse Chapel

The Polish born foundress of the Franciscan Sisters of Chicago who died in 1918 is interred in a sarcophagus at the order's motherhouse chapel. Also, on the grounds is a museum dedicated to the Apostle of Mercy from Chicago and the headquarters of the League of Mother Mary Theresa, an organization devoted to promoting her canonization. The tomb and the museum draw many visitors.

(Museum: 1:00 a.m. to 5:00 p.m. Sunday; Tomb: by appointment)

LIBERTYVILLE

158. Shrine of St. Maximilian Kolbe, Perpetual Adoration Chapel of Marytown, 1600 West Park Avenue

In 1926, the International Eucharistic Congress was held in America for the first time. To perpetuate the memory of the event in which nearly a million Catholics participated, Cardinal George Mundelein of Chicago invited the Benedictine Sisters of Perpetual Adoration to found a eucharistic sanctuary here. Mirroring the style of the nearby Archdiocesan seminary, the exterior is American Colonial. The interior decorated in marble is modeled after the Basilica of St. Paul Outside-the-Walls in Rome. Since 1972, the shrine has been under the guidance of the Conventual Franciscans of St. Bonaventure Province. In 1989, Marytown became an authorized Archdiocesan Shrine of St. Maximilian Kolbe; the friars hope it will someday be recognized as his national shrine.

(The Perpetual Adoration Chapel is open twenty-four hours a day.)

LOMBARD

159. National Shrine of Mary Immaculate, Queen of the Universe, St. Pius X Church, 1025 East Madison Street

In 1954, Pope Pius XII established the feast of the Queenship of Mary. In response, a small group of French priests, religious and lay people formed an association called L'Oeuvre De Marie Reine Immaculee "to propagate devotion to the Blessed Virgin as Queen of

Heaven and Earth." Shrines were established, the chief being at Bois-le-Roi, France. The movement spread to other countries and in Ireland the devotion came to the attention of two visiting Americans. After returning home, Eamonn and Barbara O'Malley obtained the permission of Bishop Romeo Blanchette of Joliet to establish a Marian sanctuary. On May 31, 1974, the first American shrine to Mary Immaculate Queen was dedicated. Seven years later, during the course of a public novena in honor of the Queen of the Universe, Mrs. O'Malley received the gift of healing. Since then many have been cured of their spiritual and physical maladies at the shrine. Special healing services in honor of Mary Immaculate Queen are held every Sunday.
(6:30 a.m. to 3:30 p.m.)

LOURDES

160. St. Mary of Lourdes Church

Originally called Black Partridge, this small town is the site of a large outdoor Grotto said to be an exact duplicate of the original in Lourdes, France. Built in 1928, during the pastorate of Fr. Caesar Kron, it is located on the grounds of St. Mary's Church. Constructed of colorful rocks and boulders gathered from creeks and streams by local parishioners, the grotto draws many visitors. Each year pilgrimages are held by the Lebanese people of the area and by the Blue Army. There are also outdoor Stations of the Cross.

Mailing address: c/o St. Mary Church, Metamora, IL

NORTH RIVERSIDE

161. Mother of Mothers Shrine, Mater Christi Church, 2431 South 10th Avenue

Dedicated on Mother's Day 1956, this shrine bears witness to the relationship between the Mother of Christ and mothers everywhere. Each day a special Mass is offered for all mothers giving birth that day and for all mothers that they receive all the graces necessary to fulfill their roles as mothers. Located in a suburb of Chicago, Mater Christi (meaning "Mother of Christ") is the only church by that name in the country. Devotions to the Mother of Mothers are held every Saturday morning.

ST. ANNE

162. *Original Shrine of St. Anne, St. Anne Church, 2330 North 6th Street*

Said to be the oldest U.S. shrine church honoring the grandmother of Christ, the French style structure has tall steeples and a high sanctuary. Built in 1873, it was intended for the use of French Canadians residing in the Kankakee area. People of this national background are noted for their devotion to St. Anne, so nine years later the custom of holding an annual novena to the saint began. Before long, pilgrims began to arrive from all over Northeastern Illinois. In 1894 a new relic of the saint was obtained from Rome. After venerating it on July 26 of that same year, Miss Matilda Cunnea of Chicago was cured of paralysis. Every year on St. Anne's feastday the pilgrims come as they have for over 100 years. *(8:30 a.m. until sunset)*

SPRINGFIELD

163. *St. Francis Convent, Sangamon Avenue*

Located on the spacious grounds of the motherhouse of the Hospital Sisters of the Third Order of St. Francis is an outdoor shrine to Our Lady of Fatima. Dedicated in 1953, it continues to be the goal of an annual Blue Army pilgrimage. The statues of the Blessed Virgin and the three children are white carrera marble; there is also a pond and waterfall. In a nearby niche is a smaller shrine to Our Lady of Pompeii.

One of the most famous attractions of St. Francis Convent is its Chapel of Perpetual Adoration. Built in 1935, its exterior is buff Indiana Limestone, while its interior, cruciform in shape, has attractive frescoes and is decorated with beautiful multi-colored marble. Before the exposed Blessed Sacrament, the sisters take turns praying day and night.

Also on campus is St. Francis of Assisi Church. Dedicated in 1925 and Romanesque in style, it has twin towers at the entrance and a high dome over the sanctuary. The center and heart of the church is the main altar. Built of rare marble from Greece and Italy, it is surrounded by four pillars supporting a bronze and gold-covered canopy surmounted by a crown. The church also contains a large relic of the true cross and the remains of St. Felicitas, a second century Roman martyr.

(Church — open during services only; Chapel—8:00 a.m. to 6:00 p.m.)

INDIANA

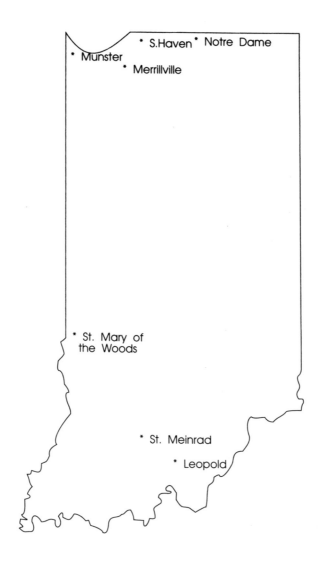

* S.Haven * Notre Dame
* Munster
* Merrillville

* St. Mary of
the Woods

* St. Meinrad
* Leopold

LAFAYETTE

164. St. Ann Church and Shrine, 612 Wabash

Weekly novena devotions to the mother of Mary began on the First Friday of 1933. That same year, an authentic relic of St. Ann was obtained from the Mother Provincial of the Sisters of Charity of Montreal, Canada. In addition to the devotions held every Wednesday evening, there is also a Solemn Novena held each year, beginning on July 18 and ending on the feast of St. Ann.
(Open during services only)

LEOPOLD

165. Shrine of Our Lady of Consolation, St. Augustine's Church

Founded by Belgian settlers, the town of Leopold is located in the southern-most part of Indiana. During the Civil War, three Union soldiers from the area were captured and placed in the infamous Andersonville prisoner-of-war camp. Lambert Rogier, Isador Naviaux and Henry Devillez vowed that if released, they would go on a pilgrimage to the Shrine of Our Lady of Consolation in Luxemburg. Rogier did make the journey and brought back a replica of the famous statue. This copy now enshrined on the left side altar of St. Augustine's Church drew many pilgrims in the past. There is also a larger outdoor statue of Our Lady of Consolation.
(7:00 a.m. to 5:00 p.m.)

MERRILLVILLE

166. The Shrine of Our Lady of Czestochowa, Salvatorian Fathers Monastery, 5755 Pennsylvania Street

One of the more interesting features of this shrine is the Panorama, a series of movable wood-carved statues portraying events in the life of Christ and various Polish saints and kings. These move to the accompaniment of commentaries, music and song in Polish and English. The shrine was founded to commemorate the 600th anniversary of Our Lady of Czestochowa and the principal focus of interest is a 8-foot by 12-foot painting of the Polish madonna by Wladek Koss. Devotions to Our Lady of Fatima — held on the second Sunday of the months May to October — are popular here, as are the annual Corpus Christi celebrations.

MUNSTER

167. Carmelite Shrines, 1628 Ridge Road

Established by a group of Discalced Carmelites from Poland, the shrine contains nearly seventy white-carrara marble sculptures and more than 250 tons of sponge rock and crystalized minerals. Begun in 1954, its most unusual feature is the Grotto. Its exterior resembles that at Lourdes but the inside is a three-story series of chapels. These interior sanctuaries honor St. Joseph, St. Anne, the Infant Jesus and our Lady of Czestochowa. Also memorialized therein are the Litany of Loreto and the Assumption. Beyond the Grotto are the Stations of the Cross culminating in the Scala Santa (Holy Stairs) leading to Calvary and the Holy Sepulchre Chapel. Also of interest are the prayer gardens; the modernistic Carmelite Church and the outdoor shrines to the Little Flower, St. Maximilian Kolbe, the Sacred Heart and Our Lady of Mt. Carmel.

(12:00 p.m. to 6:00 p.m. Sundays; other days by request)

NOTRE DAME

168. Grotto of Our Lady of Lourdes, University of Notre Dame

Christianity first came to this part of Indiana in 1686 when Fr. Claude Allouez founded the Chapel of St. Marie du Lac to serve the local Potawatomi Indians and French trappers. But 73 years later the English seized the area and expelled all Catholic clergy. It was not until 1832 that the chapel was rebuilt by Fr. Stephen Bandin, the first priest to be ordained in the United States. Ten years later, the Holy Cross Fathers were given charge of the mission. Under the direction of Fr. Edward Sorin, they built the University of Notre Dame. In 1896, with money donated by Fr. Thomas Carroll, a Marian sanctuary was built here. Composed of boulders weighing two or three tons each, it is America's most famous collegiate Lourdes Grotto. Also on campus is Sacred Heart Church with its relic of the True Cross, Bernini altar in the Lady Chapel and the nation's oldest bell carillon. Fr. Badin's body lies beneath the floor of the replica of his log chapel. Also buried at Notre Dame are Fr. Sorin, Cardinal John O'Hara of Philadelphia and Orestes Brownson.

ST. MARY-OF-THE-WOODS

169. Shrine of Our Lady of Providence, Sisters of Providence Motherhouse & St. Mary of the Woods College Campus, U.S. Highway 150 & St. Mary Road

Scipione Pulzoni, better known as Gaetano, painted the original picture of Our Lady of Providence (c. 1580). Eighty-four years later, it came into the possession of the Barnabite Fathers in the Church of San Carlo at Catinari in Rome. By 1774, the fame of this wonder-working image became so great that Pope Benedict established the Confraternity of Our Lady of Providence. Devotion to her spread to the United States in 1925 when a shrine to the Gaetano Madonna was established at St. Mary-of-the-Woods, Indiana. This Terre Haute suburb is also the American headquarters of the now Archfraternity of Our Lady of Providence. Here she is sometimes known by the secondary title of Queen of the Home.

ST. MEINRAD

170. Our Lady of Monte Cassino Shrine, Indiana Highway 62

Located one mile east of St. Meinrad Archabbey, this hill-top shrine has been drawing pilgrims for over 100 years. Named after the birthplace of the Benedictine order, the current stone structure replaces an earlier wooden one which itself superseded an open-air sanctuary. Its fame is in part due to an event which occurred during the smallpox epidemic of 1872. After several of the students at the nearby Archabbey became ill, those who still remained decided to put themselves under the protection of the Blessed Mother by making a nine-day pilgrimage novena to the Shrine. It worked! All who had the disease recovered, nor were there any new cases. Over the years, there have been a number of miraculous cures reported. Since 1932 every Sunday afternoon during May and October, pilgrims come for a Rosary procession, sermon and special prayers.

Mailing address: c/o St. Meinrad Archabbey. St. Meinrad, IN *(Open dawn to dusk)*

SOUTHHAVEN

171. Seven Dolors Shrine, Juniper Road

Comprising 160 acres of land in the northwestern part of the state, this pilgrimage center is administered by Franciscans of the Most Holy Savior Custody. The Main Grotto, from which the shrine received its name, is constructed of Tufa rock. Dominating it is a life-size statue of Our Lady of Sorrows with seven golden swords piercing her heart. Below is the sanctuary where outdoor Mass is celebrated every Sunday during summer. Circling the area is the Way of the Cross. Another grotto at the shrine is dedicated to Our Lady of Guadalupe and the Sacred Heart. Also of interest is the outdoor St. Francis Altar, encircled by Tufa and bronze representations of the Seven Sorrows of Our Lady. Finally, there is the shrine chapel with its magnificent crucifix group above the main altar.

Mailing address: 356 West 7 Mile Road Valparaiso, IN

IOWA

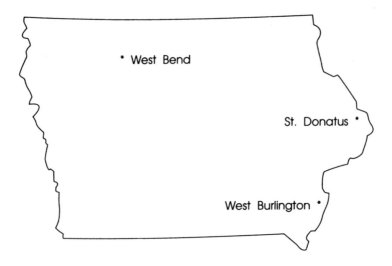

ST. DONATUS

172. St. Donatus Church, East First Street

Fifteen miles north of Dubuque, St. Donatus was founded by settlers from the Grand Duchy of Luxemburg. With many of its original limestone buildings still standing, St. Donatus retains a distinctly European atmosphere. The center of attraction in the 19th century church is a five-foot statue of Our Lady of Consolation, the Patroness of Luxemburg. As is the custom in Europe, her robes are changed to suit each liturgical season. In her hand she carries a rosary, which was a gift from Pope John Paul II. The church also has a smaller statue of the Blessed Virgin donated by the Archbishop of Luxemburg. But the principle source of St. Donatus' fame is the outdoor Way of the Cross. Built in 1861 by Fr. Michael Fammang, it was the first of its kind in the country. Winding upward on Calvary Hill are fourteen brick alcoves each containing an original Parisian lithograph detailing Christ's last journey. At the summit is the Pieta Chapel modeled after the *Chapel du Bildchen* at Vianden in Luxemburg. For those unable to make the climb up the Hill, a model of the Way of the Cross may be viewed in the parish museum.

WEST BEND

173. The Grotto of the Redemption

Beginning in 1912, and continuing until his death 42 years later, Fr. Paul Dobberstein spent all his free time in creating this three-dimensional Bible lesson. Constructed of rocks, shells, minerals and petrified materials, it covers a full square block. The nine grottos portray such subjects as the Sermon on the Mount, the Ten Commandments, the Garden of Eden and the Stations of the Cross. Trees, lawns, a lake and night illumination all combine to enhance the beauty of the display, so does the use of marble and mosaics. The Grotto continues to grow under the guidance of Fr. Louis Greving, pastor of the adjacent Sts. Peter and Paul Church. Two of the more interesting features of this house of worship are the Christmas Chapel, considered Fr. Dobberstein's finest work and the 22-foot hand carved birdseye maple altar which won first place in the

1893 Chicago World's Fair. More than 100,000 people visit the shrine each year.

WEST BURLINGTON

174. Our Lady of Grace Grotto, St. Mary Catholic Church

Begun on the eve of the Great Depression, Father M.J. Kaufman and Fr. Damien Laver built this work of Marian piety. The grotto and gardens were constructed of stones contributed by donors from every state and from many foreign countries as well. After years of neglect, the grotto was restored and improved in the 1970s by Father Jack Denning with the help of his parishioners. There are now forty varieties of trees, fountains of running water and crushed stone sidewalks. The floor, ceiling and walls of the grotto are of crystal rock. Not surprisingly, the beauty of this place attracts many visitors.

KANSAS

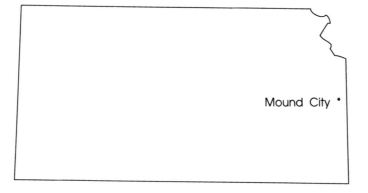

Mound City *

MOUND CITY

175. Shrine of St. Philippine Duchesne

Born in 1769, the foundress of the American branch the Society of the Sacred Heart showed an interest in missionary work among the Indians. Although she and four companions from France arrived in the United States in 1818, it was not until many years later that she realized her dream. In 1814, Fr. Pierre De Smet, the great Jesuit missionary, requested her assistance at the Sugar Creek Mission in what was then known as the Indian Territory. There Mother Duchesne worked among the Potowatomis, teaching their children, nursing the sick and spending hours in prayer. The Indians calls her "The Woman who always prays." The Shrine of St. Philippine Duchesne, a few miles from the original mission, was established on the centenary of her arrival at Sugar Creek by bishop Paul C. Schulte of Leavenworth.

Mailing address: c/o Sacred Heart Church; Mound City, KS
(Mass at 8:00 a.m. Sun. and 7:00 p.m. Thur. Open by appointment at other times.)

MICHIGAN

L'Anse * * Marquette

* Indian River

Manistee *

* Mio

Port Huron *
Grand Rapids *   Pontiac * * Sterling Hts.
Orchard Lake * * Royal
Southfield * Oak
Kalamazoo   Detroit *
* (Nazareth)
Irish Hills *

DETROIT

176. Shrine of St. Anne de Detroit, St. Anne Church, 1000 St. Anne Street

Considered by some to be the second oldest parish in the country (the oldest is St. Augustine in Florida), St. Anne was founded in 1701 by Antoine Cadillac, the famous explorer. Successive log houses of worship were constructed in 1712, 1723, and 1798. The last was destroyed, together with the whole city of Detroit in the great fire of 1905. After several years, the congregation under the leadership of Fr. Gabriel Richards, built a new stone church in 1828. The pastor, a member of the Society of St. Sulpice was one of the most outstanding figures in the early history of the state of Michigan. Father Richard's colorful career was cut short in 1832 when he contracted cholera while ministering to the victims of the epidemic. When the present church was built in 1886, his body was buried beneath the altar steps. Built in the thirteenth century Gothic Style, St. Anne's altars are of Italian marble and Mexican onyx. Administered by the Basilian Fathers, the church has five authenticated relics of the grandmother of Christ and a shrine dedicated to St. Anne. Her feast day is preceded by an annual novena. *(Open during services only)*

177. St. Bonaventure Monastery, 1740 Mt. Elliot Avenue

In the church at this Capuchin Monastery is the tomb of Fr. Solanus Casey, one of the most popular of American's candidates for canonization. Born on a farm near Prescott, Wisconsin, Casey worked as a lumberman, prison guard and trolley car operator before entering the St. Francis De Sales Seminary in Milwaukee. Several years later, he joined the Capuchin order taking his solemn vows in 1901 and being ordained a priest three years later. After serving in the New York area for twenty years, he was transferred to St. Bonaventure Monastery in Detroit where he remained until 1945. Later he lived in semi-retirement at St. Felix Friary in Huntington, Indiana for ten years. Then he returned to Detroit where he died in 1957. Fr. Solanus was noted for his piety, concern for the poor and those afflicted in body and spirit and for the efficacy of his intercessory prayer. There is a display of his memorabilia

along with a life history in photos at the offices of the Fr. Solanus guild at the Monastery.
(7:15 a.m. to 5:00 p.m.)

178. Shrine in Honor of Our Lady of Lourdes, Assumption Grotto Church, 13770 Gratiot (at McNichols)

Originally known as the church of the Assumption of the Blessed Virgin Mary, this is the second oldest parish in Detroit. Established in 1832, the log chapel did not have a resident pastor during its first twenty years. Then Rev. Amandus Vandendriesche from Belgium was appointed. During a visit to France in 1876, the new pastor visited Lourdes and was so impressed by what he saw there that he resolved to build a replica of the original grotto. Returning to the United States, Fr. Vandendriesche set to work. On May 29, 1881, the grotto was formally dedicated. Though the shrine is primarily constructed of imported limestone, the huge boulders around it were brought by farmers from all parts of Michigan. The following year, Pope Leo XIII granted partial and plenary indulgences to those who visited the grotto and prayed for the propagation of the faith. As the shrine became better known, the church began to be called Assumption Grotto. On the last Sunday in May and on August 15, many pilgrims arrived to attend services. Many miraculous cures and conversions have taken place at the shrine.
(7:00 a.m. to 7:30 p.m. M-S; 7:00 a.m. to 5:00 p.m. Sun.)

179. Rosary Shrine of St. Jude, St. Dominic's Church, 4844 Trumball Avenue

Since 1929 the rosary and prayers in honor of St. Jude have been recited daily in this Dominican staffed church. Special novena services and Holy Hours are conducted weekly at the shrine. Each year there are four Solemn Novenas.
(Open during services only)

GRAND RAPIDS

180. Sts. Peter and Paul Church, 520 Myrtle Street, N.W.

In 1941, St. Anne's popularity with the Lithuanian-Americans of the parish led to the establishment of the annual July 18th through 26th novenas in her honor.
(Open during services only)

181. St. Jude Church, 3455 Assumption Drive, N.E.

Great things can be expected from a church whose motto is "the parish with a destiny." Built in 1963, under the direction of Msgr. Charles D. Brophy, former pastor of the Catholic Shrine of Indian River, St. Jude is modernistic in style. Among its distinctive features are the bell-banner (a triangular shaped belfry above the main entrance), two Massive interior towers; the pulpit and altar of green pearl granite and the futuristic metallic sculpture titled "The Woman of the Apocalypse." Adjacent to the anthrax is the Shrine of St. Jude with its unique statue. The symbolic figure of the patron of impossible cases executed in hammered brass over solid walnut is the work of Gerald Bonnette. Novenas are held every Wednesday evening.
(9:00 a.m. to 5:00 p.m. M-S; 8:30 a.m. to 1:30 p.m. Sun.)

INDIAN RIVER

182. The Catholic Shrine, 7078 Michigan Highway 68

Blessed Kateri Tekakwitha, the Lily of the Mohawks, often erected crosses in the woods where her fellow Indians might pause to pray. This practice inspired Msgr. Brophy to established a Catholic shrine on 13 acres of donated land in this resort area. Indian River is now the site of the World's tallest crucifix. The cross carved from a single California Red wood tree is 55-feet high and weighs 14 tons. The corpus, designed by Marshall M. Fredricks, is of bronze cast in Norway. The Cross in the Woods stands on Calvary Hill at the base of which is a large outdoor church. Pilgrims approach the crucifix by ascending on their knees the Holy Stairs. Nearby is the Log-House Chapel designed by Alden Dow. Also on the grounds are the outdoor Stations of the Cross, a Madonna of the Highway shrine, the Schulmerich Carillon and a museum of religions dolls.
(Always open)

IRISH HILLS

183. St. Joseph Shrine, 8743 U.S. 12

Built in the 1850s by Irish settlers, this fieldstone structure was rebuilt and expanded in 1928. Originally resembling a schoolhouse, it now is a cruciform church with a tower and red tile roof in the California Mission style. Behind the church on the shore of Iron

Lake, Father Joseph Pferrer built the Via Crucis for which St. Joseph is famous. Commencing at the Judgment by Pontius Pilate, the stations terminate with the Crucifixion Group followed by the Resurrection. The intermediate stations are located in grottos along the Way. The Crucifixion Group is of carrara marble and weighs four tons.

Mailing address: Brooklyn, MI

L'ANSE

184. Shrine of the Snowshoe Priest

Dedicated to the memory of Bishop Baraga, Michigan's other candidate for canonization, the shrine was built in 1972. Frederick Baraga, born in Slovenia in the closing years of the 18th century, devoted his life to serving the Indians and settlers of Upper Michigan. He founded five major Indian missions, the last being at L'Anse, where he lived for ten years. Even after his appointment as the first bishop of Marquette, he continued his long winter journeys on snowshoe to visit his scattered flock. The shrine, visited by 80,000 annually, consists of a six-story high bronze sculpture of Baraga. Hand wrought, the figure holds a 7-foot cross in one hand, at his side is a 26-foot pair of snowshoes.

MANISTEE

185. St. Mary's of Mount Carmel Shrine, 260 St. Mary's Parkway

This French-style church has thousands of pounds of rough blasted white marble, Massive roof timbers and a granite altar weighing six tons. Among its attractions are the Way of the Cross — 14 oil paintings on copper slate. Also, there are twenty hand-carved statues of the Blessed Virgin, each 35-inches in height, which form a litany to the Mother of God. But the center of attention is a beautiful imported, nearly 10-feet tall, statue of Our Lady of Mount Carmel. *(8:00 a.m. to 7:00 p.m.)*

MARQUETTE

186. Tomb of Bishop Baraga, St. Peter's Cathedral, 311 Baraga Avenue

Though the present structure was built in 1939, it is the third church to occupy the site. (The first was constructed in 1853.) Located in the crypt of the cathedral are the remains of the bishop from Slovenia. A sign states "tomb of Most Rev. Frederick Baraga, D.D, first Bishop of Marquette. The Apostle to the Ottawa and Chippewa Indians, and spiritual shepherd to the Catholic pioneer settlers on the Upper Great Lakes. Died January 19, 1868. May the Lord grant to his faithful servant the honor of sainthood." His cause for canonization is presently being studied by Rome. Thousands of pilgrims visit the crypt each year.
(8:30 a.m. to 7:00 p.m.)

MIO

187. Our Lady of the Wood Shrine

The Shrine Grotto on the grounds of St. Mary Church is a mountain of Onaway stone. Dedicated in 1955, its interior holds a cave featuring the Pieta, while its exterior is honeycombed front and back with grottos and niches. Among those commemorated in these miniature shrines are the Infant of Prague, St. Anne de Beaupre, the Holy Family and St. Francis. Also, the Blessed Virgin is shown in a series of grottos honoring her by five of her best known titles: Our Lady of Fatima, Lourdes, La Salette, Guadalupe and Czestochowa.
(8:00 a.m. to 5:00 p.m.)

NAZARETH

188. Chapel of the Agony, Sister of St. Joseph Motherhouse, Nazareth Center (Northeast Kalamazoo)

In a smaller sanctuary to the rear of the Holy Family Chapel on the grounds of Nazareth College, is the Scala Sancta. The Holy Stairway erected in 1913 is similar to the one in Rome. It represents the stair case our Lord ascended and descended at the court of Pontius Pilate. Encased in each of the twenty-eight steps are relics

from the Holy Land. Those seeking the indulgence, mount the stairs on their knees.
(8:00 a.m. to 8:30 p.m. M-F; 8:30 a.m. to 8:30 p.m. Sat.; 9:30 a.m. to 8:30 p.m. Sun.)

ORCHARD LAKE

189. Shrine-Chapel of Our Lady of Orchard Lake, Orchard Lake Schools

Founded in 1885 in Detroit by Fr. Joseph Dabrowski, the schools were transferred here in 1909. The Shrine-Chapel, built in 1963, is intended as a place of worship for the students and as a place of pilgrimage for Polish-Americans. Dominating its facade is the 25-foot tall image of Our Lady of Orchard Lake, said to be the largest copper statue of its kind in the world. Inside, all attention is focused on the altar made of imported light and dark gray Botticino-classic marble. In addition to the shrine-altar dedicated to Our Lady of Czestochowa and the Immaculate Conception, there are side chapels devoted to the Virgin of Guadalupe and five Polish Madonnas. The latter are those of Kozielska, Ostrobrama, Piekarska, Swarezewska, and Zebrzdowska of Calvary, Poland.
(Always open)

PONTIAC

190. Shrine of the Immaculate Heart of Mary, St. Joseph Church, 400 South Boulevard

Every First Saturday, Detroit Catholics come here to honor the Immaculate Heart of Mary. Since 1948, there has been an annual Pilgrimage Festival. Featured are a holy hour and an outdoor Mass followed by a long procession of banner-carrying parish groups from all over southeastern Michigan and beyond. Founded in 1924, St.Joseph was enlarged and renovated fifteen years later. After seeing a statue of Our Lady of the Cape in the Chapel of Peace during the 1947 Marian Congress in Ottawa, Canada, Fr. B. F. Jarzembowski obtained a similar one with a gold heart. This he placed on a shrine-altar dedicated to the Immaculate Heart. The following year, the annual pilgrimage began. Later, outdoor Stations of the Cross were erected and in 1952, a Grotto-Chapel

adjoining the church on the east side was completed. In it was placed an Italian marble statue of the Sorrowful and Immaculate Heart of Mary. It said that eight years later on the Feast of the Queenship of Mary, the image came to life briefly. Her eyes opened, she gazed at the witnesses with love, and tears of joy ran down her cheeks.
(Open during services only)

PORT HURON

191. St. Edward's On-The-Lake, 6945 Lakeshore Road
Devotion to Our Lady of Fatima came to this parish with the arrival of Fr. John R. Hogan as pastor in 1950. Twenty-five years later Bishop John Venacio of Leira-Fatima, Portugal blessed St. Edward's famed outdoor shrine of Our Lady of Fatima. The following year, Archbishop Fulton J. Sheen preached a well-attended novena. After the disastrous fire of 1984, the flow of pilgrims has diminished somewhat but they still arrive by the busload. Each Sunday there is a Holy Hour of Reparation; Our Lady of Perpetual Help devotions are held on Thursday evenings and the King of Divine Mercy is honored by an annual novena.
Mailing address: Lakeport, MI
(7:30 a.m. to 2:00 p.m.)

ROYAL OAKS

192. The Shrine of the Little Flower, 2123 Roseland
The octagonal-shaped church, founded by Fr. Charles Coughlin, the now retired radio priest, is fronted by the Crucifix Tower, each side of which forms a cross. Constructed between 1929 and 1933, the exterior walls are ornamented with stones carved with the state flower of each state in the Union. The interior of the 3,000 seat church centers on the 18-ton white carrara marble main altar, considered the largest monolithic altar in the country. In addition, there are noteworthy side chapels honoring Our Lady, St. Joseph, St. Sebastian and St. Perpetua. But the focal point of each pilgrimage is, of course, a visit to the shrine-chapel of the Little Flower. Monumental oak doors weighing 700 pounds each open into a room large enough to serve as a church for weekday Masses. Its walls are of Travertine marble with inserts of black Belgian

marble. Dominating the chapel is the altar of St. Therese which portrays the saint receiving a rose from the Child Jesus seated on His Mother's lap.

(7:00 a.m. to 3:30 p.m. M-F; 8:00 a.m. to 7:30 p.m. Sat.; 7:00 a.m. to 3:00 Sun.)

SOUTHFIELD

193. St. Anthony Shrine, Duns Scotus Friary, 20,000 West Nine Mile Road

The heart of the complex of buildings called Duns Scotus is the chapel. Built in 1930, and dedicated to St. Anthony of Padua, the Gothic cruciform structure is modeled after the Basilica of San Francisco in Assisi, Italy. Beneath a beautiful Lombard baldachin (canopy) stands the main altar made of Siena gray marble. Entered through a gate at the south of the sanctuary is the Chapel of St. Anthony. In a niche above the mensa altar is a colored wood statue of St. Anthony holding the Divine Infant. To the left is a reliquary holding relics of this popular saint. Devotions to St. Anthony are held every Tuesday night. Once a month, the Franciscans hold a Day of Renewal.

(6:30 a.m. to 5:00 p.m.)

STERLING HEIGHTS

194. Our Lady of Czestochowa Church, 3000 Eighteen Mile Road

Administered by priests of the Society of Christ, this church in suburban Detroit is intended to be a monument to the Black Madonna of Jasna Gorna. Built and consecrated in 1982, Cardinal Edmund Szoka refers to it as "Czestochowa in Detroit." The church has an icon blessed by Pope John Paul II and touched to the original in Poland. Not surprisingly, all liturgies are in Polish.

(Open during services only)

MINNESOTA

* Onamia

* St. Cloud

Cold Spring *   * Isanti

* New Ulm

Sleepy Eye *

COLD SPRING

195. Assumption Chapel

After grasshoppers had ravaged southwestern Minnesota for two summers in a row, Fr. Leo Winters, O.S.B. suggested that the parishioners of Jacob's Prairie and St. Nicholas make a pledge to the Blessed Virgin. If she would halt the yearly infestation, the farmers would build a chapel in honor of the Assumption and offer frequent Masses there for fifteen years. The vow was made, and the grasshoppers disappeared. So in 1877 a frame chapel was erected and a statue of the Virgin and Child enshrined in it. But the shrine was destroyed by a tornado seventeen years later, though the statue of Our Lady was saved. For many years the site continued to be a place of pilgrimage for local Catholics but it was not until 1951 that a new stone chapel was built. Resting on a wooden hill, the *Gnaden Kappelle's* exterior is of rough pink granite and a single steeple rises over it. Above the entrance is a plaque showing the Blessed Virgin ascending into heaven while grass-hoppers below bend their knees in homage. The interior is of granite. The imported stained glass windows portray a selection of Our Lady's titles. Above the altar is the original Marian statue now repaired and restored.

Mailing address: c/o Church of St. Boniface; 418 Main Street, Cold Springs, MN
(Open daylight hours, April to November)

ISANTI

196. St. Elizabeth Seton Church

On the grounds of the church is a Rosary Shrine constructed in 1983. It consists of an enclosed area containing a life-sized crucifix and a statue of the Blessed Virgin. Our Lady stands on a pedestal in a raised garden in the loop of large stone beads portraying the five decades of the rosary. The Bishop of St. Cloud designated the shrine as a place of pilgrimage during the Marian Year of 1987-1988.

NEW ULM

197. The Way of the Cross, 1324 Fifth, N.

On land which they then owned, Sister Favia and the Poor

Handmaids of Jesus Christ completed the Way of the Cross in 1904. Visitors begin by praying at a shrine depicting the Agony in the Garden, then follow a gravel path leading upward past each station (brick structures enclosing imported Bavarian sculptures representing scenes from the Passion of Christ). Midway up Loreto hill is a Lourdes Grotto. At the summit, on a bluff overlooking the city and the Minnesota River is a chapel to Our Sorrowful Mother. Located adjacent to Sioux Valley Hospital, the shrine, now owned by the diocese of New Ulm, is cared for by the Knights of Columbus.

ONAMIA

198. National Shrine of St. Odilia, Crosier Fathers' Seminary

Sometime during the 4th century, St. Odilia and her companions having set out for the East, fell into the hands of evil men and were martyred at Cologne. Years passed; then in 1287, the saint appeared to Brother John, told him that she would be the Patroness of the Croisiers and indicated where she was buried. After they were recovered, her relics were kept at the order's motherhouse at Huy, Belgium but were lost during the French Revolution. It was not until 1949 that St. Odilia's remains were returned to the order. Three years later, the seminary at Onamia obtained one of her major relics. A shrine was established in her honor as Patroness of the Blind. Novenas are held there twice a month, beginning on the 5th and 17th. A national novena is held each year from July 10 until her feast day on the 18th.
(Daylight hours)

ST. CLOUD

199. St. Mary's Cathedral, 25 Eighth Avenue S

The history of this episcopal center began in 1855 with the building of the first St. Mary's. The present church, constructed in 1931, is the third. Six years after its completion, the Romanesque structure was designated as the cathedral for the newly created Diocese of St. Cloud. St Mary's has a long history of devotion to Our Lady of Perpetual Help. Though the chapel in the lower church dedicated to her was destroyed by fire in 1987, novenas in her honor continue. And there are plans to rebuild the shrine. Also, in a specially designated area in the crypt church is a statue of the patron of the diocese.

(8:00 a.m. to 10:00 p.m. Tue.; open during services on other days)

SLEEPY EYE

200. Schoenstatt Shrine

An exact replica of the original shrine of Our Mother Thrice Admirable Queen and Victress of Schoenstatt, Germany, the Sleepy Eye sanctuary is one of eighty such scattered throughout the world. Located on the shores of one of the beautiful lakes for which Minnesota is famous, it was constructed in 1976. Five years later, a retreat center was added.

(6:00 a.m. to 9:00 p.m.)

NEBRASKA

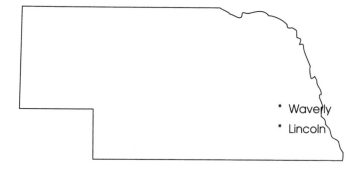

LINCOLN

201. Eucharistic Shrine of Christ the King, 1040 South Colner Boulevard

Christ the King Church is the officially recognized Eucharistic Shrine of the Diocese of Lincoln. It is maintained by the Holy Spirit Adoration Sisters who because of the color of their habits are known as the Pink Sisters. The Blessed Sacrament is exposed all day, every day. Among the daily adorers are members of two lay organizations: the King's Men and the Ladies of the Eucharist.

(Always open)

WAVERLY

202. Kalin Memorial Tower, Catholic Center

Donated by Mr. and Mrs. Leander Kalin, the 90-foot tower has an attached outdoor altar surmounted by a large statue of the Blessed Virgin. Around it are stone block carvings of the Way of the Cross. Designed by Albert Hamersky, the Marian shrine was dedicated in 1964 by Cardinal John Ritter of St. Louis. Also at the Catholic Center three miles west of Waverly are the Good Counsel Retreat house, Villa Marie School and the motherhouse of the Marian Sisters.

NORTH DAKOTA

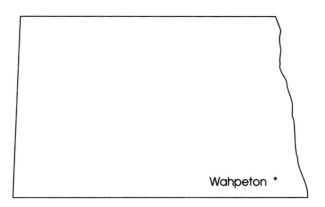

Wahpeton *

WAHPETON

203. Shrine of Our Lady of the Prairies, Carmel of Mary, Route 5

When the monastery for the Carmelite Nuns was founded, Cardinal Aloysius Muench expressed his desire that there be a public shrine to the Blessed Mother. In fulfillment of his wish, an outdoor sanctuary was erected in honor of Our Lady of the Prairies. Here she is depicted as walking barefoot through a wheat field holding a sheaf of wheat. The annual pilgrimage, held since 1957, takes place in August on the Sunday closest to the Solemnity of the Assumption. Large crowds gather for evening Mass and the rosary procession.

OHIO

Genoa *

Carey *

* Bellevue

* Marywood   Parma

*

Euclid *

* Cleveland

* Garfield
Hts. * Chagrin Falls

Bedford *   * Welshfield

* N. Jackson

Youngstown *

Canfield

Randolph *

Canton *

Massillon *

Russells Pt. *

*

Maria Stein

* Steubenville

* Dayton

* Cincinnati

* Fatima

BEDFORD

204. Our Lady of Levocha Shrine, Villa San Bernardo, 1160 Broadway, Route 14

For centuries, some say as many as 700 years, pilgrims have been coming to Marianska Hora (Marian Hill) in the Tatra Mountain region of Slovakia. On this holy mount near Levocha, there is now a beautiful Neo-Gothic church dedicated to Our Lady of the Visitation. To perpetuate this old-country devotion, the Vincentian Sisters of Charity built the shrine to the Slovakian Madonna in 1930. Presiding over the outdoor sanctuary, is an exact replica of the wonder-working statue of Our Lady of Levocha. The official pilgrimage season extends from the first Sunday in May to the first Sunday of October. The high point is July 2, the feast of the Slovakian Virgin.
(Daylight hours)

CANFIELD

205. St. Anthony's Wayside Shrine, St. Paul Monastery, Route 224

Founded in 1944, the shrine, located on a busy highway, draws visitors from all over the country. Thousands more participate by mail. The Wayside Shrine, staffed by the priests of the Society of St. Paul, is famous for its novenas to St. Anthony of Padua and Mary, Queen of the Apostles. The emphasis on the Franciscan saint is a response to popular demand. Devotion to our Lady by the above title is one of the distinctive features of the Pauline Fathers, an order devoted to spreading the Gospel using the modern communications media. The statue of the Queen of the Apostles was designed by Sr. Angelica Billari of the Disciples of the Divine Master, a Pauline order.
(Always open)

CANTON

206. Our Lady of Lourdes Grotto, Central Catholic High School, 4824 Tuscarawas St. West, U. S. Route 172

The shrine, located on the grounds of the former Mount Marie Academy, was built using stones from every state in the Union.

There are also pebbles and rock fragments from the Garden of Gethsemani, from Nazareth, from the Holy Sepulchre and from the Rock of Massabielle. Planned and built by Sr. Paula Nentwick and the Sisters of Humility of Mary, the Grotto had drawn thousands to Marian Masses and devotions.

CAREY

207. The Basilica and National Shrine of Our Lady of Consolation, 315 W. Clay St.

Originally called St. Edward, the church was renamed Our Lady of Consolation in honor of the patroness of Luxemburg from which country many of the area's first settlers came. In 1875 a copy of the famous Madonna was obtained from the Grand Duchy. When it arrived, over 1,000 people gathered at the parish rectory in Berwick, and under the leadership of Father Joseph P. Gloden, carried the statue in procession to Carey, seven miles away. It is reported that though there was a sudden downpour, none of the pilgrims were touched by the rain. Father Gloden and his diocesan successors enthusiastically fostered devotion to Our Lady of Consolation, as did the Conventual Franciscan who were later given charge of the parish. Eventually the old church proved too small to hold the ever growing number of pilgrims. A new site was chosen and construction began. Dedicated in 1925, by Bishop Samuel Strich of Toledo, the new church has been designated both a National Shrine and a Basilica. The red brick Romanesque style structure is cruciform in design. The exterior boasts a tall, slender bell tower and a huge rose window above the triple arched entrance. The church has a seating capacity of 2,600. The shrine altar of Our Lady of Consolation is to the left of the main altar. The Luxemburg Madonna has a septer in her right hand while her left holds the Child Jesus who is depicted as bestowing a blessing. Both Mother and Child are crowned and wear beautiful robes which change with the liturgical season. Near the church are several buildings similar in style and material to it. One, called Pilgrims' House, is a hotel operated by the Sisters of St. Francis for the benefit of those who wish to stay overnight or for an extended period. In addition, the thirty landscaped acres hold a large

outdoor shrine to the Luxemburg Madonna, a Way of the Cross and various small shrines and grottos.
(Always open)

CHAGRIN FALLS

208. Shrine of Our Lady of Perpetual Help, St. Margaret of Hungary Church, 4680 Lander Road

The shrine to the Blessed Mother is located on grounds once occupied by a home for the aged run by the Daughters of the Divine Redeemer. The site has been owned by St. Margaret of Hungary Church since 1971. Each Sunday from May until October there are two Masses at the shrine: the Hungarian Mass at noon and the English liturgy at 1:00 p.m. A popular celebration is held in conjunction with the feast day of St. Stephen, the beloved first Christian king of Hungary.

CINCINNATI

209. National Shrine of St. Anthony, St. Anthony Friary, 5000 Colerain Avenue

In 1897 a monastery and chapel were built to serve as the novitiate for the St. John the Baptist Province of the Franciscan Order. The chapel, though dedicated to St. Anthony of Padua, was not intended to be a shrine but as the years passed, it became one. In the mid 1920s, the Third Order of St. Francis began annual public pilgrimages to the chapel. Every Tuesday there are devotions to the Saint from Padua. Particularly popular is the Novena of Nine Tuesdays before June 13, (St. Anthony Day.)
(6:00 a.m. to 9:00 p.m. Tue.; 6:00 a.m. to 6:00 p.m. other days)

210. Holy Cross-Immaculata Church, 30 Guido Street, Mount Adams

Situated on Mount Adams overlooking the city and the Ohio River, the Immaculata, was built in 1859 by Archbishop John B. Purcell. It was intended as a permanent memorial to the proclamation of the dogma of the Immaculate Conception five years before. Also located here is Holy Cross church built in 1895. Both are

administered by the Passionists. Every Good Friday, pilgrims climb the 180 steps up Mount Adams. Some say a Hail Mary on each step and one Our Father on each of five landings. On reaching the summit, pilgrims venerate the cross. This popular devotion has been in existence for over 100 years.
(7:00 a.m. to 7:30 p.m.)

CLEVELAND

211. St. Paul's Shrine of Perpetual Adoration, Conversion of St. Paul Church, 4120 Euclid Avenue

Archbishop Joseph Schrembs' desire to have a center for eucharistic worship for his archdiocese found its fulfillment with the purchase of the former Episcopalian Church of St. Paul in 1930. The new church, now under the guidance of the Capuchin Friars, was renamed the Conversion of St. Paul. To it the archbishop attached a monastery of Poor Clares of Perpetual Adoration whom he had brought from Austria. These cloistered nuns are at prayer before the Blessed Sacrament all day and all night (except during Mass or other services). The popular Gothic style shrine has an Altar of Adoration of carrara marble flanked by two groups of adoring angels. The gilded monstrance stands on an elevated throne under a peaked canopy. Nearby in the chapel of Our Mother of Mercy stands an exact replica of the miraculous statue of Our Lady of Altoetting from Germany.
(Open during services only)

DAYTON

212. Our Lady of Lourdes Grotto, Bergamo Center, Mount St. John, 4435 East Patterson Road

Brother Michael Mertes' dream was to build a memorial honoring the Blessed Virgin's eighteen appearances to St. Bernadette Soubirous. The site was to be a property owned by the Society of Mary at Bergamo/Mt. St. John where he was the Assistant Novice Master. From his fellow Marianists in France, he obtained the exact measurements of the original Lourdes grotto and the Franciscans of Washington D.C. provided a perfectly-proportioned model of it. With the help of his novices and a group of Italian-American workmen from Chicago, the shrine was built in 1929. It remains a popular place of pilgrimage.

EUCLID

213. Shrine and Grotto of Our Lady of Lourdes, 21320 Euclid Avenue (U.S. Route 20)

The idea for building this Marian sanctuary occurred to Mother Mary of St. John Berchmans McGarvey while visiting the motherhouse of the Good Shepherd Sisters in France. On returning to the United States, she set to work raising funds for the project. Located on a hill overlooking Lake Erie in suburban Cleveland, the shrine was dedicated in 1926. Two years later, on the occasion of a city-wide pilgrimage, Archbishop Schrembs of Cleveland conferred on the grotto the title of the "National American Shrine of Our Lady of Lourdes." Since then many thousands have visited this sanctuary and numerous favors, spiritual and temporal, have been reported. The waters of the spring nearby are considered to have healing powers. Since 1952, the shrine has been under the care of the Sisters of the Most Holy Trinity whose Novitiate and Provincial House are located here.

FATIMA

214. Our Lady of Fatima Shrine (near Ironton)

Built under the guidance of Fr. Louis A. Phillips during the Marian Year of 1954, the shrine is located on a 250 foot by 350 foot plot of donated land in rural Lawrence County. Entering through an arched gateway, the visitor sees before him a landscaped area in the center of which is a pond. On an island is a group of statues depicting Our Lady's appearance at Fatima, Portugal. Toward the rear are a series of mosaics honoring the fifteen mysteries of the rosary. The shrine is maintained by the Watterson Council of the Knights of Columbus.

GARFIELD HEIGHTS

215. Our Lady of Czestochowa Shrine, Provincial House of the Sisters of St. Joseph of the Third Order of St. Francis, 12215 Granger Road

Situated on the spacious campus of the Marymount Provincial convent, the Marian sanctuary was dedicated in 1939. Enshrined within the Byzantine style chapel is a replica of the original image from Poland. There is an annual pilgrimage on the Sunday nearest the feast of the Assumption, August 15. Also on the grounds is the Sacred Heart Wayside Shrine built in 1960 in cooperation with Fr. F. Larkin and the National Enthronement Center.
(Open dawn until dusk)

GENOA

216. Our Lady of Lourdes Grotto, Our Lady of Lourdes Church, 204 Main Street

When Bishop Karl Alter of Toledo visited the shrine at Lourdes, France in the summer of 1932, he vowed to build a similar grotto in his diocese. Two years later, while visiting Genoa at the invitation of Father Stephen Jazwiecki, a site was chosen. In less than two months, volunteers from the parish of Our Lady of Lourdes completed construction of the Grotto using one million pounds of tufa from Castalia, Ohio. The material used is not rock but mineral coated petrified vegetation. The statues of the Blessed Virgin and St. Bernadette were donated by Bishop Alter. The shrine was dedicated on September 8, 1934.

MARIA STEIN

217. Shrine of the Holy Relics, Sisters of the Precious Blood, 2291 St. John Road

When Fr. J. M. Gartner visited Rome in 1872, Italy was in turmoil. Churches and convents were being looted and sacred relics were filling the windows of pawn shops. Fr. Gartner set out to rescue as many sacred articles as possible. With the help of a number of influential people, he aMassed an outstanding collection of relics.

Returning to the United States, he exhibited them in several cities to enthusiastic throngs. At the suggestion of Cardinal John McClosky of New York, he decided to keep the accumulation intact. So, in 1875, he donated the relics to the Sisters of the Precious Blood who enshrined them in their Adoration Chapel. Because of the ever growing number of visitors, the Shrine had to be enlarged twice. Finally in 1892, a new chapel was built. Meanwhile, the collection was increasing; Rev. Francis de Sales Brunner and Archbishops John McNicholas and Karl Alter (both of Cincinnati) each made substantial additions, as had Pope Pius IX. The hilltop chapel now holds what may be one of the largest collections in the world. Included are relics of the true cross, of the life and death of Christ and of the Blessed Virgin, the apostles and a seemingly endless galaxy of saints and martyrs.
(9:00 a.m. to 5:00 p.m.)

MARYWOOD

218. Sorrowful Mother Shrine, 4106 State Route 269

In a wooded area which reminded him of a famous Marian shrine in the Black Forest in Germany, Father Francis Brunner built a small red-brick chapel in honor of Our Lady of Sorrows in 1850. In it he placed a hand carved wooden statue of the "pieta" type. Before long, pilgrims began arriving and miraculous cures were reported. By 1870, the chapel had become too small and was replaced by a larger German Gothic edifice. But in 1912 the structure, together with the wonder-working image, burned to the ground. Undiscouraged, the Precious Blood Fathers rebuilt the shrine and replaced the original statue with a Daprato composition sculpture of the Sorrowful Mother holding her dead Son. Pilgrims still come to this first Marian sanctuary in the Midwest. An outdoor Way of the Cross was added in 1915. And twenty-three years later a Lourdes grotto was built. There followed the erection of the shrines honoring the Fatima apparition, Our Lady of Guadalupe, St. Francis and St. Clare. In 1968, the outdoor Pieta Chapel was built.

Mailing address: Bellevue, OH
(9:00 a.m. to 5:00 p.m.)

MASSILLON

219. National Shrine of St. Dymphna, Massillion State Hospital, 3000 South Erie Street

According to legend, the patron saint of those afflicted with mental and nervous disorders was a 7th century Irish princess. After the death of her mother, she and her confessor St. Gerebran fled to Belgium to escape from her pagan father. But the king followed them to Gheel and demanded that she marry him. When she refused, she and the priest were slain. The bodies were hastily buried and the site of their graves soon forgotten. But in the 13th century their remains were rediscovered and placed in the local church. St. Dymphna's fame spread when it was noticed that many spectacular cures of the insane, epileptics and the possessed occurred through her intercession. Located on the grounds of Massillion State Hospital, the National Shrine under the direction of Fr. Matthew M. Hettna, was the first church in America to be dedicated in her honor. Novenas to St. Dymphna are said daily.
(8:00 a.m. to 4:30 p.m. M-F)

NORTH JACKSON

220. National Shrine of Our Lady of Lebanon, 2759 North Lipkey Road

Dedicated in 1958, the Maronite shrine is a replica of one founded fifty years earlier in Harissa, Lebanon. The focal point of the 80 acre sanctuary is the shrine tower. Surmounting it is a 16 foot, 7 1/2 ton granite statue of the Blessed Virgin as the Immaculate Conception, patroness of Lebanon and the United States. Encircling the tower and the chapel housed within it, is a stairway which leads the pilgrim up to the Mother of God. Nearby are the Glass Chapel, Cedars Hall and the new chapel dedicated to Christ, the Prince of Peace. Vespers to Our Lady of Lebanon is held every Wednesday evening. Her feast is the first Sunday in May. Another popular day of pilgrimage is August 15, Assumption Day. The shrine is operated by the Eastern Rite Diocese of St. Maron.
(9:00 a.m. to 5:00 p.m.)

PARMA

221. Queen of the Holy Rosary Shrine, Incarnate Word Academy, 6618 Pearl Road

Facing the well traveled road between Columbus and Cincinnati on U.S. Route 42, the shrine was sure to draw the attention of travelers. Built in 1936 by an anonymous donor, the outdoor Marian sanctuary boasts a majestic statue of the Madonna and Child carved from a single block of wood by a skilled Bavarian craftsman. A pilgrimage is held each year in May to the shrine on the campus of the Motherhouse of the Sisters of the Incarnate Word and the Blessed Sacrament.

RANDOLPH

222. Our Lady of Lourdes Shrine, St. Joseph Church, 2643 Waterloo Road

One of the oldest parishes in the state, St. Joseph had already been in existence for ten years when St. John Neumann arrived here to reorganize it in 1841. The present church, built in 1905, is the fifth to serve this community of German-Americans. In 1927 Fr. Edward Spitzig built the Lourdes Shrine for which the church is famous. Masses are said at the grotto every Saturday evening from Memorial Day to Labor Day. A Triduum including Mass, rosary, candlelight procession and Benediction is held every August 13, 14, 15 in the evening.

Mailing address: Mogadore, OH

RUSSELLS POINT

223. Our Lady of Fatima Shrine

Maintained by the American Society of Ephesus, the Marian sanctuary has been called Ohio's best kept secret. From within her 43-foot high shrine, the Virgin of Fatima gazes across Indian Lake. The statue itself is the largest of its kind in the world. At night, concealed black lights illuminate her, while fifteen fountains of ever changing color dance to religious music. The statue, which makes a complete revolution every thirty minutes, can be seen for miles. The shrine may be visited during the daytime. (Night illumination is limited to the Summer months.) There is a pilgrimage each year on October 13, the feast day of Our Lady of Fatima.

Mailing address: American Society of Ephesus (George B. Quatman Foundation), 327 North Elizabeth Street, Lima, OH

STEUBENVILLE

224. Portiuncula, Franciscan University of Steubenville

While visiting the birthplace of the Franciscan Order in Assisi, Italy, Fr. Sam Tiesi, T.O.R. was inspired to build a replica of St. Francis' famous chapel on the campus of this Ohio college. Sixteen feet in width and 34 feet long, the shrine is just large enough to hold twenty pews and a small tabernacle. Currently open for prayer and meditation, plans call for perpetual adoration at the Chapel.
(6:00 a.m. to 12:00 Midnight)

WELSHFIELD

225. Our Lady of Mariapoch, 17486 Mumford Road

In November 1696 in the village church of Poch, Hungary, the icon of the Blessed Virgin began to shed tears. By order of the Emperor, the painting was taken to Vienna, the capital of the Austrian Empire. Two years later, through the intercession of the Hungarian Madonna, the city was saved from the Turks. A copy of the original icon kept at Poch (now called Mariapoch) wept three times during August 1715. Over the centuries, the fame of Our Lady of Mariapoch has increased. In 1956, a shrine to the Hungarian Weeping Madonna was established on 50 acres of wooded land in a suburb of Cleveland. On the Sunday closest to August 15, an annual Pilgrimage is held. Every Sunday a special devotion to the Miraculous Weeping Madonna of Mariapoch is conducted.

Mailing address: Burton, OH
(11:00 a.m. to 9:00 p.m. Sundays)

YOUNGSTOWN

226. Our Lady, Comforter of the Afflicted Shrine, Our Lady of Cziksomlyo Chapel, Mt. Alvernia Friary, 517 South Belle Vista Avenue

For more than 400 years, pilgrims have been coming to the Marian sanctuary at Cziksomlyo in the Transylvania region of Rumania. When the Franciscans who operated the shrine were driven out by the Soviets in 1948, the refugees came to the United States. Here they worked among American Hungarian Catholics, many of whom were immigrants also. In 1963, the Friars received permission to build a new monastery and a replica of their old country shrine from the Bishop of Youngstown. In it they placed a copy of the centuries old miraculous statue of Our Lady, Comfort of the Afflicted of Cziksomlyo.

(7:00 a.m. to 8:00 p.m.)

SOUTH DAKOTA

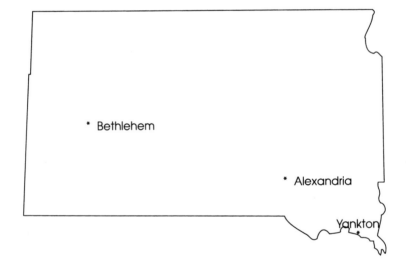

ALEXANDRIA

227. Fatima Family Shrine, St. Mary of Mercy Church

At the time of the Miracle of the Sun at Fatima, Portugal, the three children and many others witnessed the appearance of the Holy Family in the sky. Some have taken this as a call for the sanctification of family life. One such person was Fr. Robert J. Fox who built the Fatima Family Shrine on the grounds of St. Mary of Mercy Church. Dedicated in 1987 by the bishop of Leira of Fatima, Portugal, the shrine's most famous feature is the four outdoor granite sanctuaries. Within the quartet of stone alcoves are marble statues depicting our Lady of Fatima, St. Joseph with the Child Jesus, the Sacred Heart and an Angel adoring the Eucharist. Nearby is the Holy Family Chapel, the Pro-life Shrine in honor of Our Lady of Guadalupe that was dedicated and blessed by Cardinal Edouard Gagnon, Prefect of the Vatican's Council on the Family. Also nearby is the specially sculpted marble statue of the Angel of the Family of and of Youth. Young married couples stop at the Holy Family Chapel to consecrate their marriages to the Immaculate Heart of Mary. Families also come to consecrate themselves to her care. An annual National Marian Congress is held at the shrine the third weekend of each June, which draws pilgrims from throughout the United States and other countries.

Mailing address: Alexandria, SD

BETHLEHEM

228. Shrine of the Nativity

In 1952, a generous donor gave the Benedictine Fathers a small parcel of land in the Black Hills region of South Dakota. Realizing that the property was honey-combed with caverns, the monks under the direction of Fr. Gilbert Stack, set to work to build a replica of the place where Jesus was born. Visited by 10,000 people a year, the Shrine of the Nativity is located in a crystal cave on the upper level of Bethlehem Cave. Marking the spot and visible for miles is the five story carillon tower.

(9:00 a.m. to 5:30 p.m.)

YANKTON

229. House of Mary Shrine, Highway 52

Situated on the shore of Lewis and Clark Lake, this Marian
sanctuary owes its origin to a local group called the Rosary Makers.
Begun in 1971, the shrine has a Way of the Cross winding up
Calvary Hill. The 13th station consists of three 50-foot wooden
crosses which when lighted at night are visible for miles. Other
attractions include the Rosary Pond, a Meditation Area, the Scala
Santa, the Rosary Way and the Chapel of St. Joseph. There are small
shrines honoring St. Benedict, the Infant of Prague, St. Anne, St.
Isadore and the Little Flower. Also, scattered about the grounds are
statues of Mary, Moses, the Risen Christ, St. Michael and St. Joseph.
(9:00 a.m. to 8:00 p.m.)

WISCONSIN

Ashland *

* Hurley

Champion *

DePere *

Polonia *
Rudolph *

* Hubertus
Waukesha * * Milwaukee

Madison *

* Palmyra

* Burlington

* Dickeyville

* Twin Lakes

ASHLAND

230. St. Francis Shrine, St. Agnes Catholic Church, 106 Second Avenue, E.

Under the guidance of Father Andre Schludecker, O.F.M., local volunteers constructed this homage to the Poor Man of Assisi. Dedicated in 1985, the log cabin style chapel behind St. Agnes church overlooks Chequamegon Bay on Lake Superior. Among the sights which greet pilgrims is an 8-foot white pine statue of the founder of the Franciscan order. Nearby sits a wooden image of the wolf of Gubbio tamed by St. Francis.

(9:00 a.m. to 9:00 p.m.)

BURLINGTON

231. St. Francis Monastery and Retreat Center, 503 South Brown's Lake Drive

It was the shrine-altars of Our Lady of Ostrabrama and the Black Madonna of Czestochowa in the chapel of this Franciscan Friary that first attracted outside attention. Soon, pilgrims of Polish descent from Milwaukee and elsewhere began coming. Among the notable features of the shrine are a Calvary scene surrounded by the Way of the Cross, a Lourdes Grotto, an outdoor shrine to Our Lady of Czestochowa and a replica of St. Francis' Portiuncula complete with a San Damiano cross.

(Open sunrise to sunset)

CHAMPION

232. Shrine of Our Lady of Good Hope, Chapel House of Prayer

It is believed by many that in 1859 the Blessed Virgin appeared three times to Adele Brice a 28-year-old Belgian immigrant. On the third of these occasions, the Lady said "I am the Queen of heaven who prays for the conversion of sinners . . . if they do not convert and do penance, my Son will be obliged to punish them . . . gather the children . . . and teach them what they should know for Salvation . . . teach them their catechism." Shortly after, a log chapel was built near the scene of the apparitions. Two years later, it was replaced by a frame chapel; a school and convent were added later. Then in 1871,

Door Peninsula and much of southeastern Wisconsin went up in flame in the great Pestigo Fire. But the shrine was miraculously saved. To meet the needs of the increasing number of pilgrims, a new brick chapel was built nine years later. Then in 1895, the Norbertine Fathers, in order to combat a schismatic group of "Old Catholics," inaugurated the annual May Pilgrimage. The shrine, which was rebuilt in 1933, is now administered by the Sisters of St. Francis of Bay Settlement. Each year, on August 15, there is a pilgrimage Mass, often celebrated by a bishop.

Mailing address: New Franklin, WI
(7:00 a.m. to 9:00 p.m.)

DE PERE

233. National Shrine of St. Joseph, St. Norbert Abbey, 1016 North Broadway

In 1888, ten years after the church was founded, Fr. Joseph F. Durin of the Missionaries of the Sacred Heart became pastor. This priest was zealous in the promotion of the patron of the Universal Church. He initiated the Perpetual Novena to St. Joseph and arranged for the solemn coronation of his statue. When the church was destroyed by lightning and fire, Fr. Durin rebuilt the church in 1890. Following his departure and death, the shrine was given into the care of the Norbertines who had come to this country from Holland. The new director, Abbot Bernard H. Pennings, proved to be just as dedicated to St. Joseph as his predecessor had been. With the completion of St. Norbert Abbey in 1959, the Archconfraternity of St. Joseph and the crowned statue of the head of the Holy Family found a new home. The perpetual novena to St. Joseph is held every Wednesday evening.

(Open dawn to dusk)

DICKEYVILLE

234. Dickeyville Grotto, Holy Ghost Church, 305 Main Street

The shrine in the southwestern part of Wisconsin is the work of Fr. Matthias Wernerus who became pastor of the red-brick, single-spired Church of the Holy Ghost in 1918. His first project was the erection of a Crucifixion Group honoring the war dead of the

parish. Then he began work on the grotto using thousands of bits of stone, china, colored glass, petrified wood, shells, carnelian and other bright objects. Next, with the assistance of his parishioners and the local school children, he constructed a series of smaller grottos depicting in stone, marble and concrete the Sacred Heart, the Blessed Virgin, the Twelve Apostles and the Tree of the Holy Ghost. Thousands of pilgrims visit the shrine each year.
(Open day light hours)

HUBERTUS

235. Shrine of Our Lady of Holy Hill, State Highway 167, 1525 Carmel Road

There is a legend that Fr. Marquette, the famous explorer, was the first to plant a cross on the summit of this lofty hill. Perhaps it was this story that led Roman Goetz to erect a 15-foot white oak cross here in 1858. Five years later, to accommodate the pilgrims who were coming in increasing numbers, a log chapel was built. Later the shrine's famous statue of Mary, Help of Christians was installed. On that occasion, eighteen maidens bore the Marian image on the 8-mile journey from St. Hubertus Church in Hubertus, Wisconsin. The procession was accompanied by 100 horsemen and several hundred enthusiastic pilgrims. Soon the chapel was too small, and in 1881 a larger one was built. Fifteen years later, the shrine came under the direction of the Discalced Carmelites from Bavaria. They built the nearby monastery and constructed the present six-story church in 1938. Its exterior is German Gothic in design with a great rose window and two high-pointed towers. The interior is Romanesque. The latest addition is the shrine chapel built in 1956. In it resides the now more than 100-year-old statue of Mary, Help of Christians. Bavarian in origin, the image shows Our Blessed Mother gazing down toward the Divine Child who raises his hand in blessing. Fourteen life-size scenes from the passion form the half-mile long Way of the Cross along the old tree-lined road that leads to the church.
(6:00 a.m. to 7:00 p.m.)

HURLEY

236. St. Mary of the Seven Dolors Church, 404 Iron Street

Built in 1886, the church's title reflects the tragic fires and mining accidents that have occurred in the area. Within, one finds a larger-than-life statue of Our Lady whose heart is pierced with seven swords of sorrow. Each Friday parishioners and people from the neighboring community of Ironwood, Michigan gather for a novena service honoring Our Sorrowful Mother. And there is an annual commemoration on September 15, the feast of Our Lady of Sorrows.

MADISON

237. Schoenstatt Heights, 3601 Highway BB

There are four places in Wisconsin where Our Mother Thrice Admirable of Schoenstatt, Germany is venerated. The shrine at Madison, built in 1953, was the first in the state and the first in the country. Originally located on the grounds of Queen of the Apostles Seminary, it was moved to its present site on a hill overlooking the state capitol when the center for training priests closed in 1979. *(8:00 a.m. to 6:00 p.m. Winter; 8:00 a.m. to 8:00 p.m. Summer)*

MILWAUKEE

238. Archdiocesan Marian Shrine, 217 North 68th Street

Before turning over responsibility to the Archdiocese of Milwaukee, the Dominican Sisters of the Perpetual Rosary cared for the shrine for about twenty years. Located at the corner of 68th and Stevenson, its "heart" is a grotto-like reconstruction of the apparition of Fatima. To the right are a small chapel and base reliefs of the mysteries of the rosary in groups of five. A memorial plaque is on the left. Every 13th of the month from May to October, there is an evening Mass, Rosary and candlelight procession. Each Sunday afternoon, the rosary is recited at 2:00 p.m.

239. Holy Cross Church, 5424 West Bluemound Road

On the grounds of the church is an exact replica of the famous Marian shrine of Schoenstatt, Germany. It is one of two in

Milwaukee. Fr. Joseph Kentenich, founder of the Schoenstatt Movement, said daily Mass here from 1954 until 1965. He built the Holy Cross shrine in 1954.
(6:30 a.m. to 8:00 p.m.)

240. Mariengarten Shrine, St. Philip Neri Church, 5566 North 68th Street

Dedicated in 1962, the other Milwaukee Schoenstatt shrine was built by Fr. Ahler, pastor of the church. Mass is celebrated here on weekdays. The Schoenstatt Sisters of Mary administer the sanctuary and also teach at the parish grade school.
(8:00 a.m. to 8:30 p.m.)

PALMYRA

241. World Shrine of Our Lady of Green Scapular

The Blessed Virgin in an apparition to Sister Justine Bisqueyburau, promised that this sacramental would contribute to the conversion of souls, particularly those who have no faith. In 1955, Fr. Jerome Mersberger obtained permission from the bishop of Madison to found a shrine honoring Our Lady of the Green Scapular. Originally in Madison, it was moved to Palmyra in 1968. The sanctuary houses a statue of the Blessed Virgin by Jose Ferriera Thedim called the 20th century's greatest sculptor by Pope Pius XII. The shrine also has a relic of Mary: a small piece of her veil or scarf. There is also a Green Scapular Museum nearby. Both are open by appointment only.

POLONIA

242. Our Lady of the Sacred Heart Shrine, St. Clare Convent

John Trzebiatowski built a shrine to the Blessed Virgin under this title on the grounds of the Felician Sisters convent. As time went by, the Marian sanctuary began to develop a small but devoted clientele. During one of the novenas to Our Lady, the prayers of the mother of a bride-to-be were answered. On the day of the wedding the daughter changed her mind, little knowing that she had been about to marry a bigamist. News at the favor spread and the shrine began attracting

more attention. Eventually it became too small and with the assistance of August Pudroski, it was enlarged. But by 1974, its size was again inadequate and a new shrine built under the guidance of Sister Mary Pontia and Sister Mary Stanisia.
(8:00 a.m. to 6:00 p.m. Summer; 9:00 a.m. to 4:00 p.m. Winter)

RUDOLPH

243. St. Philip's Grotto Shrine, 6957 Grotto Avenue

While visiting Lourdes, France, Fr. Philip J. Wagner promised the Blessed Virgin that if his prayers for better health were answered, he would build a shrine in her honor. After recovering his health, the pastor of St. Philip's church spent all of his spare time for thirty-one years building this sanctuary. The first to be constructed was, of course, the Lourdes Grotto. There followed the Wayside Shrine; the Wondercave with its numerous miniature shrines; the Chapel of St. Jude made of hand cut logs; the Sunken Gardens and Lily Pond and the Patriotic Shrine, his homage to God and country. Edmund Rybicki continues the work begun by Fr. Wagner.

TWIN LAKES

244. La Salette Shrine, 10330-336th Avenue (HWY KD)

On September 19, 1846, the Blessed Virgin appeared to two children near La Salette in the French Alps. She spoke of the need to change people's hearts through prayer and sacrifice and of the chastisements that would follow if people did not change their ways. It was to spread this message that the Missionaries of Our Lady of La Salette was founded. One of the apostolates of the order is the staffing of Marian sanctuaries. The shrine at Twin Lakes is the only one in the midwest dedicated to the Virgin of La Salette. Featured is a tableau telling the story of the French apparition in stone.

WAUKESHA

245. Schoenstatt Center, W 284 North 698 Cherry Lane

The first mention of St. Michael Chapel at Schoenstatt, Germany dates from 1319. Since then the Marian sanctuary has been destroyed and rebuilt twice, eventually coming into the hands of the Pallottine Fathers. On October 18, 1914 Fr. Joseph Kentenich and a group of students from the nearby Seminary entered into a covenant of love with the Blessed Virgin. This was the beginning of the Schoenstatt Movement of renewal and Marian devotion. Since then the original chapel has become a center of pilgrimage. There are now more than eighty sanctuaries dedicated to Our Mother Thrice Admirable, Queen and Victress scattered over five continents, each an exact replica of the mother shrine at Schoenstatt. The one at Waukesha, founded in 1964, serves as the U.S. headquarters for the movement. *(6:00 a.m. to 8:30 p.m.)*

PART THREE: SHRINES OF THE SOUTH AND WEST

Alabama
Alaska
Arizona
Arkansas
California
Colorado
Florida
Hawaii
Idaho
Kentucky
Louisiana
Maryland
Missouri

Mississippi
Montana
New Mexico
Nevada
North Carolina
Oklahoma
Oregon
Tennessee
Texas
Virginia
Washington, D.C.
West Virginia

ALABAMA

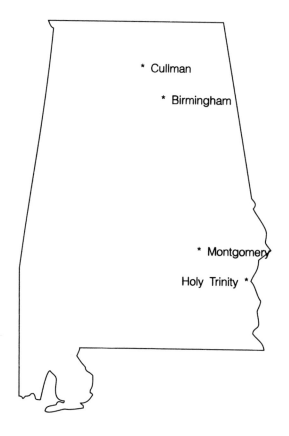

* Cullman

* Birmingham

* Montgomery

Holy Trinity *

BIRMINGHAM

246. The National Shrine of St. George, St. George the Great Martyr Melkite Greek Catholic Church, 425 Sixteenth Avenue, S

The Melkites are Catholics who use Masses rituals of Antioch rather than those of Rome. St. George's has the distinction of being the first Eastern Rite church in the world to use English in its liturgy. In 1979, the Melkite Patriarch elevated it to the status of a national shrine. The church has two icons and a relic of the martyr.
(Open during service only)

CULLMAN

247. Ave Maria Grotto, St. Bernard Abbey, 600 St. Bernard Drive, S.E.

Alabama's only Benedictine Monastery was established in 1892. Among its first residents was Bavarian born Brother Joseph Zoettl whose hobby was making miniature replicas of famous churches and shrines. His models became so popular with visitors to the monastery that an area was set aside for their exhibition. Brother Joseph continued his work until his death in 1961. Today more than 120 miniatures are spread over three scenic acres. Among the shrine's attractions is the Marian Grotto, a 20-foot deep cave cut into a hillside. Its walls and ceiling are decorated with artificial stalactites and a life-size statue of the Blessed Virgin with St. Benedict and his sister St. Scholastica.
(7:00 a.m. to sunset)

MONTGOMERY

248. St. Jude Church, City of St. Jude, 2048 West Fairview Avenue

Founded by Passionist Fr. Harold Purcell, the city of St. Jude is one of the largest institutions in the country serving the spiritual, medical, educational and social needs of the poor. The heart of the 56-acre complex is St. Jude Church built in 1938. The red brick building with its 100-foot bell tower and blue tile roof can be seen for miles. Modeled after Santa Maria Church in Rome, the interior is a lesson in catechetics. The Ten Commandments are portrayed on the ceiling cross beams and the Creed and Sacraments on the glass windows. There is an annual novena to St. Jude in October. *(8:00 a.m. to 5:00 p.m.)*

HOLY TRINITY

249. Blessed Trinity Shrine Retreat

When Fr. Thomas A. Judge arrived in the state in 1915, he found widespread poverty and lack of education. As a result he founded, with the assistance of Margaret Louise Keasey, a school for the children of the poor. From the small group of volunteers which the work attracted, a new order of sisters emerged: the Missionary Servants of the Most Blessed Trinity. Their motherhouse was located here until 1930. Thirty-six years later, the Blessed Trinity Shrine Retreat was dedicated. The sisters' original chapel and Fr. Judge's log cabin have been preserved. Since the early days there has been a pilgrimage in honor of the Blessed Virgin on the Feast of the Assumption.

(Always open)

ALASKA

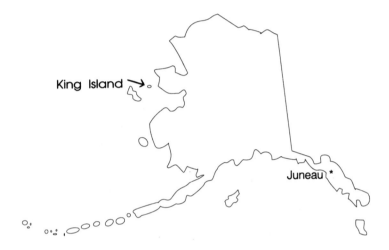

JUNEAU

250. Shrine of St. Therese

The shrine is situated on State Highway 7, 23 miles from the center of Juneau. It was dedicated in 1914 by Bishop Joseph R. Crimont, the first bishop of Alaska. (The bishop was later buried within his beloved church). The shrine is located on a small island connected to the mainland by a causeway. A bronze statue of St. Therese of Lisieux (the Little Flower) stands before the church.

Mailing address: 56933 Lund Street, Juneau, AK
(9:00 a.m. to 9:00 p.m. Summer; 9:00 a.m. to 6:00 p.m. Winter)

KING ISLAND

251. Christ the King

High on a hill, on an island in the Bering Sea, Fr. Bernard Hubbard, S.J., the "Glacier Priest" erected a 900-pound bronze statue of Christ the King in 1937. The island received its name on that occasion when the Catholic Eskimo inhabitants dedicated themselves and their homes to the Messiah. Pilgrimages are still made to the statue by the natives of the area.

ARIZONA

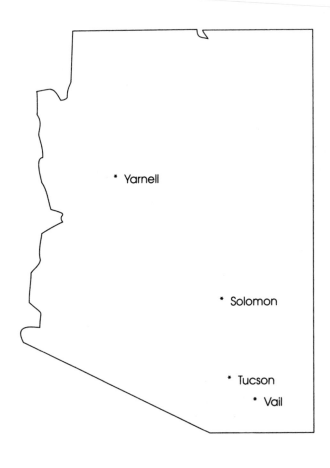

SOLOMON

252. Shrine of Our Lady of Guadalupe, Our Lady of Guadalupe Church

Though the history of the parish goes back more than 100 years, the present church was built in 1911. Seventy years later, to mark the 450th anniversary of the Mexican apparition, the Diocese of Tucson selected Our Lady of Guadalupe Church as a place of pilgrimage. The following year, the church was designated a historic site. Each day a rose is presented to the Blessed Virgin by a parishioner. This is called the "Living Rose" devotion.
(6:00 a.m. to 5:00 p.m.)

TUCSON

253. Mission San Xavier del Bac, San Xavier Road

Called by the Indians *La Paloma del Dieserto* (White Dove of the Desert), the church is considered the most beautiful of all the Spanish Missions. Founded in 1700 by the famous Jesuit missionary Fr. Eusebio Kino, the present church was built by the Franciscans during the years 1783-1797. To the left of the sanctuary, in the Chapel of the Suffering Savior is the reclining figure of the greatest of the Jesuit missionaries. The image on the sepulchre represents the incorrupt body of St. Francis Xavier which can still be seen in Goa, India. The Arizona statue has been the goal of many pilgrimages; many cures have been attributed to the saint's intercession.
(9:00 a.m. to 6:00 p.m.)

VAIL

254. Shrine of Saint Rita in the Desert

Built in 1945 by Mrs. Charles Beach, the church is dedicated to St. Rita of Cascia, the 15th century Italian saint known as the Patroness of Desperate Cases. The shrine is relatively small, seating only eighty to 100 people. The Salvatorian staffed church has an altar carved from the stones of the Santa Rita Mountains, and a statue of St. Rita imported from Italy. Many pilgrims come here, especially in the Spring and Fall.
(6:00 a.m. to 6:30 p.m.)

YARNELL

255. Shrine of St. Joseph of the Mountains, U.S. Highway 89

Located a half mile west of town, the shrine dedicated to the foster father of Jesus was founded by the Catholic Action League of Arizona in 1939. Its famous outdoor statues, many of them life-size, are made of reinforced concrete and are the work of Felix Lurero of Tucson. The first sculpture to be completed was that of St. Joseph. He is depicted holding carpenter's tools in one hand and carrying the Holy Child in the other. Among the shrine's numerous other sculptures are those depicting the Last Supper, the Agony in the Garden, the Way of the Cross and the Crucifixion.

(Always open)

ARKANSAS

* Winslow

* Little Rock

LITTLE ROCK

256. Discalced Carmelite Monastery of St. Theresa, 7201 West 32nd Street

In 1950, at the invitation of Bishop Albert L. Fletcher, the first group of contemplative nuns arrived in this Southern Protestant city. The present monastery was built eleven years later — after the first was damaged by a bomb during Little Rock's school integration crisis. Every July, the Catholic churches of the area — including the cathedral — sponsor a novena of Masses in honor of Our Lady of Mt. Carmel at the sister's chapel. There is also a novena to St. Joseph in March.
(6:00 a.m. to 6:00 p.m.)

257. Our Lady of the Holy Souls Church, 1003 North Tyler Street

In the early part of the 18th century the Blessed Virgin is said to have appeared to Sister Clare Isabella Fornari. She promised to grant a particular tenderness and devotion to all who venerate her as Our Lady of Confidence. The original image painted by Carlos Maratta, is at the Poor Clare Convent at Todi, Italy. There is a famous copy of it in the chapel of the Pontifical Major Seminary in Rome. Devotion to the "Fiducia" as she is known, spread to this country by American graduates of the school. Her popularity was greatly aided by the 1941 deathbed recovery of a Dominican sister in Grand Rapids, Michigan. The principle U.S. center of devotion to Our Lady of Confidence is this modern style church built in 1971.
(Open during services only)

WINSLOW

258. Our Lady of the Ozarks Shrines, U.S. Highway 71

The native stone structure built in 1941 was established to serve the needs of the Catholic residents of the Boston Mountains area in the Ozarks. Within the church is a shrine-chapel with a life-size statue of the Blessed Virgin holding a rosary. There is an annual celebration featuring a procession and the crowning of the outdoor statue of Our Lady of the Ozarks. The famous image stands on a pedestal facing U.S. Highway 71. Popular with tourist and pilgrims alike, the church is open from morning until nightfall.

CALIFORNIA

ALTADENA

259. Lourdes of the West, St. Elizabeth Church, 1849 North Lake Avenue

Following the canonization of St. Bernadette, worldwide attention was focused on the events of her life and especially on the apparitions to which she had been a witness. With this in mind, Fr. Corr commissioned Louis Kado, a fifth generation Japanese-American rock artist, to create a replica of the original French shrine on the grounds of St. Elizabeth Church. In the construction of the 25-foot grotto dedicated in 1939, 130 tons of lava rock from the Mono Lake area, along with tons of concrete and steel reinforcement were used.

CARMEL

260. Mission San Carlos Borromeo, 3080 Rio Road

Founded in 1770, the Mission was the second established in Alta California by Bl. Junipero Serra and served as his headquarters. He and Fr. Lousen, the actual builder of the church are buried beneath the floor of the sanctuary. When visiting the restored Mission, one may view Fr. Serra's cell where his Bible and other belongings are on display. The church is also a center of veneration of Our Lady of Bethlehem, a devotion originating in 15th century Portugal. The beautiful statue of her enshrined here is a gift from the Archbishop of Mexico City given prior to the Mission's founding. The church was raised to the rank of a minor basilica in 1960.
(9:30 a.m. to 4:30 p.m.)

LAKE ARROWHEAD

261. Our Lady of Fatima Shrine, Our Lady of the Lake Church, 27462 Rim of the World Drive

Because the outdoor shrine is positioned directly behind the main altar of the church and the sanctuary wall is glass, those within may clearly view it while attending Masses. The shrine is a statuary group carved by Jose Thedim, who sculpted the statues at Fatima. The artist was one of those who witnessed the Miracle of the Sun on October 13,

1917. The rosary is said each day and there are special Marian devotions in May and October.

Mailing address: Crest Park, CA

LATON

262. Shrine of Our Lady of Fatima, 20855 Fatima Ave.

Located in an area with a high concentration of immigrants from Portugal, the church was founded in 1953 by Fr. Joseph P. Lima, a native of the Portugese Azores Islands. As might be expected, the parishioners are very devoted to Our Lady of Fatima, the patroness of that country. Each year in May, Portugese speaking pilgrims flock to Laton for a special celebration in her honor.

(8:00 a.m. to 8:30 p.m. MF; 4:00 p.m. to 6:30 p.m. Sat.; 8:00 a.m. to 1:00 p.m. Sun.)

LINCOLN

263. Shrine of Our Lady of Guadalupe, Third and K Streets

The capilla (chapel of Spanish architecture) was built in 1957 by the Hispanic people of the area to honor the patroness of Mexico. Above the main altar is a large oil painting of Our Lady of Guadalupe. There is a monthly First Friday Masses in Spanish, preceded by the rosary.

Mailing address: c/o St. Joseph Church, 585 D street, Lincoln, CA
(Open during services only)

LOS ANGELES

264. Our Lady of the Rosary of Talpa Church, 2914 East 4th Street

The state of Jalisco in Mexico has two famous shrines: one at Zapopan and the other at Talpa. The latter owes its fame to a 17th century legend concerning the miraculous restoration of a statue of Our Lady of the Rosary after it had been badly burned. This white stucco edifice built in 1946 by the Vincentians is the only church dedicated to Our Lady of Talpa in this country. Within there are two images of the Mexican Madonna: a replica of the original statue and a painting by the Alejandro Pardinas, the famous Spanish artist.

There is an annual novena in her honor prior to September 19, her feast day.
(8:00 a.m. to 6:00 p.m. M-F, use side entrances)

265. Santuario de Nuestra Senora de Guadalupe, 4100 East Second Street

Thousands of Mexican-Americans and other Hispanics attend the ten Masses celebrated here each Sunday. People from the parish and from all parts of East Los Angeles and beyond come to pray to St. Lawrence (San Lorenzo), Our Lady of San Juan de Lagos, St. Martin de Porres and Our Sorrowful Mother (La Soledad). The Holy Child of Atocha, St. John the Evangelist and St. Jude are also popular. The principle devotion is, of course, to Our Lady of Guadalupe. The 12th of each month is celebrated in her honor. And all look forward to her feast day in December.
(7:00 a.m. to 7:30 p.m.)

REDWOOD VALLEY

266. Holy Transfiguration Monastery, 17001 Tomki Road

Staffed by the Monks of Mt. Tabor of the Ukrainian-Byzantine Rite, the monastery is a place of pilgrimage for Eastern Rite Catholics who come to venerate the famous Icon of Our Lady of Mt. Tabor. Dedicated in 1983, the shrine houses an Eastern style painting of the *Hodegetria* type done by Dominic Tarrish of San Francisco. Pilgrims report receiving many special, sometimes miraculous, graces here.
(Always open)

SACRAMENTO

267. National Shrine of Our Lady of Guadalupe, 711 T Street

Founded in 1958 as a chapel or mission of the Cathedral of the Blessed Sacrament, Guadalupe Church was elevated to a parish eleven years later. Considered the spiritual home of the Hispanics and Mexican Americans in northern California, it was declared a national shrine in 1978. (Twelve years earlier, the march of Cesar Chavez and the Farm Workers to the State Capital climaxed here when demonstrators handed to Bishop Alden J. Bell the cross and

candle they had carried all the way from Delano.) In 1968, Pope Paul VI sent a 24-karat gold rose mounted on a marble base with the papal coat-of-arms to the church. The current pastor is also the first Hispanic auxiliary bishop of the diocese.
(Open during services only)

SAN DIEGO

268. St. Jude's Shrine of the West, 1129 South 38th Street
Novenas to the Saint of the Impossible are held periodically. Chartered buses come from as far away as Los Angeles, San Bernardino and Riverside. Each year the statue of St. Jude is carried in procession through the streets.
(8:00 a.m. to 6:00 p.m. M-S; 7:00 a.m. to 7:00 p.m. Sun.)

SAN FRANCISCO

269. Shrine of St. Jude Thaddeus, St. Dominic Church, 2390 Bush Street
Began in 1935 by Father William Thomas Lewis, novenas to the patron of difficult and seemingly impossible cases have become a tradition at this Dominican church. Under the directorship of Fr. Patrick D. Kane, the shrine expanded rapidly from a purely local devotional center to a sanctuary whose influence is national. There are seven novenas a year, the most popular of which is the one in October that ends on the feast of St. Jude.
(6:30 a.m. to 5:30 p.m. M-S; 6:30 a.m. to 8:00 p.m. Sun.)

SAN JUAN CAPISTRANO

270. Shrine of St. Peregrine, Old Mission San Juan Capistrano, 31522 Camino Capistrano
Every year on March 19, St. Joseph's Day, the swallows return to this Spanish mission founded by Bl. Junipero Serra. The adobe chapel which he constructed in 1776 has been restored. As a result of the miraculous cure of a cancer stricken parishioner, the mission has become a shrine to St. Peregrine. A novena in his honor is held every Saturday morning.
(7:30 a.m. to 5:00 p.m.)

SANTA CLARA

271. Mission Santa Clara de Asis, Santa Clara University

Born in 1761 at Montblanch, Spain, Magin Catala entered the
Franciscan order at age seventeen. After ordination, he volunteered
for the missions of America. At length he was assigned to Mission
Santa Clara de Asis where he spent the next thirty-six years of his
life. Here he became known for his piety, austerities and zeal for the
evangelization of the California Indians. Witnesses claimed that once
when praying before a crucifix, Fr. Catala was lifted from the floor,
and while still elevated was embraced by Jesus. He died in the odor
of sanctity in 1830. His body has been interred in the Crucifix chapel
in the restored Mission Church on the campus of Santa Clara
University. The first steps toward his canonization have been taken.
(8:00 a.m. to 6:00 p.m.)

272. Shrine of Our Lady of Peace, 2800 Mission College Boulevard

The focal point of this Marian sanctuary adjacent to State
Highway 101 is a 32-foot, 7,200-pound stainless steel statue of the
Blessed Virgin. Commissioned by Fr. John Sweeny, pastor of Our
Lady of Peace Church, and constructed in sculptor Charles Park's
studio in Delaware, the statue was exhibited first at Wilmington,
Philadelphia and Chicago. Dedicated in 1983, the shrine features
First Friday all-night vigils, perpetual adoration, weekly holy hours
and Fatima devotions on the 13th of each month, May through
October. The October devotion reproduces the identical ceremonies
of Fatima with candlelight rosary procession and blessing of the sick.

SANTA CRUZ

273. St. Joseph's Shrine, 544 West Cliff Drive

In 1952, construction began on the shrine located on the grounds
of what was once the seminary of the Oblates of St. Joseph. But due
to lack of funds, work stopped after the completion of the crypt
church. Recently, new funds were discovered and progress
subsequently began again. Novenas to the stepfather of Jesus are
conducted Monday through Friday after the 11:00 a.m. Masses. The

devotion of the "Seven Sorrows and Joys of St. Joseph" is recited every Wednesday.
(6:00 a.m. to 7:00 p.m.)

SANTA MONICA

274. St. Anne's Shrine, St. Anne Church, 2051 Colorado Avenue

Situated on the grounds of the church is an outdoor sanctuary and pavilion dedicated to the grandmother of Jesus. Devotion to St. Anne has been an important feature of parish life since its beginning in 1908. Each year there is a popular Solemn Novena to the mother of Mary from July 18 to 26. Perpetual devotions to St. Anne are held each Wednesday in the church.

SYCAMORE

275. Shrine of Our Lady of Sorrows

Colusa Country's first Masses was an outdoor one, held at this exact site. Eight years later, in 1864, Fr. La Fauber conducted a mission here, at the close of which a 27-foot wooden cross was erected. Masses, pilgrimages and visits continued; in 1883 a small brick chapel dedicated to Our Lady of Sorrow was built. The Shrine, renovated in 1922 and again in 1979, has been placed in the National Register of Historic Places. Each year in the springtime a pilgrimage Masses is celebrated.

Mailing address: c/o Our Lady of Lourdes Church, 745 Ware Avenue, Colusa, CA

COLORADO

* Golden

* Pueblo

* Silverton

San Luis *

* Trinidad

GOLDEN

276. Mother Cabrini Shrine

The hills of Mt. Vernon Canyon held a special attraction for the first American saint; she purchased land here. During one of her visits to the site, using locally obtained white rocks, she fashioned the image of a heart — in honor of the Sacred Heart — near the summit of a mountain. The grotto honoring Mother Cabrini erected in 1929 was replaced thirty years later by a modernistic chapel with a seating capacity of 100. A 22-foot high statue of the Sacred Heart, dedicated in 1954, now stands in front of Mother Cabrini's white rock heart. The 383 steps leading to it are flanked by Stations of the Cross and the Rosary Pathway.

Mailing address: Missionary Sisters of the Sacred Heart of Jesus, Golden, CO

(6:30 a.m. to 7:30 p.m. Summer; 6:30 a.m. to 5:30 p.m. Fall-Spring)

PUEBLO

277. St. Therese Church, 300 Goodnight Street

When the Diocese of Pueblo was founded, Bishop Joseph C. Willging named St. Therese of Lisieux as its patroness and this church was intended as her shrine. However, lack of funds prevented the erection of a ground level church, so the crypt became the parish church. The statue of St. Therese stands at the rear. Eventually a new church will be built with a separate shrine chapel.

(5:00 a.m. to 6:00 p.m.)

SAN LUIS

278. Sangre de Cristo Church

Adjacent to the adobe edifice, built in the 1880s and served by the Theatine Fathers, is a grotto honoring Our Lady of Guadalupe. Also nearby is a museum dedicated to the *Hermanos Penitentes* and a hillside Way of the Cross featuring near-lifesize bronze figures. A retreat center is planned.

TRINIDAD

279. Ave Maria Shrine, John F. Kennedy Drive

Located on the grounds of Mt. San Raphael Hospital on a hillside overlooking Trinidad, the shrine's origin is shrouded in mystery. The French-manufactured statue of Our Lady of Grace which is its focus has been there since 1908. At some later time, a grotto of native stone was built. Then in 1934 the Circolo Mariano Society led by Rosaria Vecchia began building the present grotto and chapel. The project was not completed until shortly before the end of World War II. While the shrine was under the care of the Third Order of St. Francis, outdoor Stations of the Cross, a 50-foot metal cross and a statue of the saint from Assisi were added. The Marian sanctuary is currently operated by Holy Trinity Church in Trinidad.
(Open during services only)

SILVERTON

280. Christ of the Miners

On the east slope of Mount Anvil, high above the town of Silverton, stands this monument to the faith of the miners of southwestern Colorado. During the 1950s most of the lead mines in the area had closed and the local economy was depressed. The men of St. Patrick's Church decided to erect a shrine in the hope that prosperity would then return. Under the leadership of Fr. Joseph Holleran, the sanctuary was completed in the summer of 1959. Twenty-four feet high and 40-feet wide at the base, it contains a 16-foot, 12-ton statue of the Sacred Heart of Jesus imported from Italy. A few months after the completion of the shrine, uranium was discovered and prosperity soon returned.

FLORIDA

St. Augustine *

Orlando *

* St. Petersburg

Miami *

MIAMI

281. Shrine of Our lady of Guadalupe: Patroness of the Unborn, 18340 N.W. 12 Avenue

Erected in 1981, the outdoor shrine is located next to the Respect Life Office of the Archdiocese of Miami. Our Lady is depicted wearing a black band around her waist, the sign that Mexican Indian women wore to show that they were with child. Outdoor Masses are celebrated here periodically throughout the year.

282. Our Lady of Charity Shrine, 3609 South Miami

La Virgin de la Caridad, as she is called in Spanish, is the patroness of Cuba. Devotion to her began in the late 1500s when two men and a boy, having been spared from death during a tropical tempest, discovered her statue floating near their boat. This Marian sanctuary was constructed at the request of Archbishop Coleman F. Carroll of Miami who donated the land on which it stands. Dedicated in 1973, the edifice is conical in form, 90-feet high and 80-feet wide. The focal point of the Shrine is a replica of the statue honored at El Cobre, Cuba. Behind the image of Our Lady of Charity is a mural depicting the history of that troubled land by Teok Carrasco. The feast of the Cuban Virgin is celebrated on September 8.
(9:00 a.m. to 9:00 p.m.)

ORLANDO

283. Mary, Queen of the Universe Shrine, 8300 Vineland Avenue

Located near Disneyworld and Epcot Center, the shrine is likely to be popular with visitors to central Florida. Founded by Fr. F. Joseph Harte, the Marian sanctuary is being constructed in two phases, the first of which was completed in April 1986. Located on the 17-acre site are a temporary church which seats 600, a bell tower and courtyard, lawn and garden areas, offices, fountains and a reflecting pool. If all goes well, the second phase will be completed in 1992. Plans call for a larger 2,000 seat church, an audio-visual theater and a museum of religious art.
(9:00 a.m. to 5:00 p.m.)

ST. AUGUSTINE

284. Shrine of Our Lady of La Lache, Mission Nombre de Dios, San Marco Blvd

Fifty-five years before the Pilgrims landed at Plymouth, the first Masses in St. Augustine was celebrated at the site of what was to become *Mission Nombre de Dios* (Name of God). From here for two centuries Jesuit and Franciscan missionaries went forth to spread the Gospel to the Indians to the north and west. It is fitting that St. Augustine, which is the first permanent Catholic settlement in America, is also the location of the first U.S. Marian shrine. In 1620, Spanish settlers built a chapel at the mission and dedicated it to *Nuestra Senora de La Leche y Buen Parto* (Our Nursing Mother of Happy Delivery). Enshrined within is a replica of Our Lady of La Leche, the original of which is in the Church of San Luis in Madrid. The image depicts the Blessed Mother nursing the Divine Child. Many an expectant mother has prayed here for a safe delivery and a healthy child. The shrine has been destroyed several times. The present chapel dates from 1915. The principal pilgrimage day is September 8, the birthday of Our Lady. Also on the grounds are the Way of the Cross, the Mysteries of the Rosary, the Prince of Peace Church and the Beacon of Faith. The latter is a 70-ton stainless steel cross dedicated in 1966 by the Archbishop of Madrid. At 208 feet, it is said to be the tallest in the Western Hemisphere.
(8:00 a.m. to 6:00 p.m.)

ST. PETERSBURG

285. Cathedral of St. Jude, 5815 5th Avenue, N.

Dedicated in 1950, this Florida parish has grown considerably over the years. In 1968 when the Diocese of St. Petersburg was founded, St. Jude Church was chosen as its cathedral. A perpetual novena to the Patron Saint of Difficult and Hopeless Cases is conducted every Monday. The service consists of Masses, novena prayers and the application of the relics of St. Jude.
(10:00 a.m. to 3:30 p.m.)

HAWAII

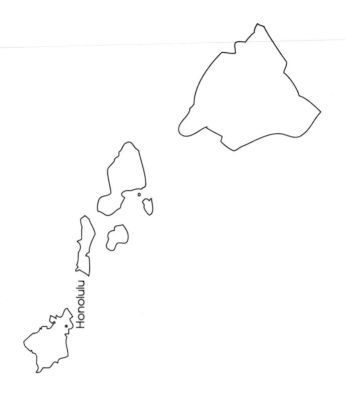

Honolulu

HONOLULU

286. Our Lady of Peace Cathedral, 1184 Bishop Street

Built in 1843 of native coral blocks, the cathedral is the oldest Catholic church in Hawaii. At its entrance is a plaque honoring Fr. Damien de Veuster, the leper priest of Molokai, who was ordained here. In its courtyard stands the gold leaf painted statue of Our Lady of Peace erected in 1893, said to be a copy of a more ancient image venerated in France. There is an annual feast day celebration in honor of the Hawaiian Madonna on July 9th.
(6:00 a.m. to 6:00 p.m.)

IDAHO

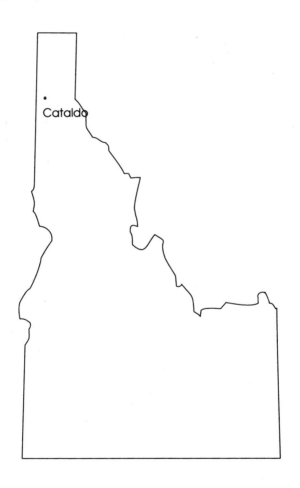

CATALDO

287. Sacred Heart Mission

Administered by the Idaho State Park Commission, the "Old Mission" is the goal of an annual pilgrimage by the Couer d'Alene Indians on August 15. Designated a National Landmark, the church is Idaho's oldest building. Constructed by the Indians in the 1850s, the wooden structure's white pillared front has a high scalloped gable decorated with a great rayed host in gold and enamel. Later boundary changes left the church outside the reservation and the Indians moved to a new mission at De Smet, Idaho. But each year they return.

(8:00 a.m. to 6:00 p.m. Summer; 9:00 a.m. to 5:00 p.m. Fall-Spring)

KENTUCKY

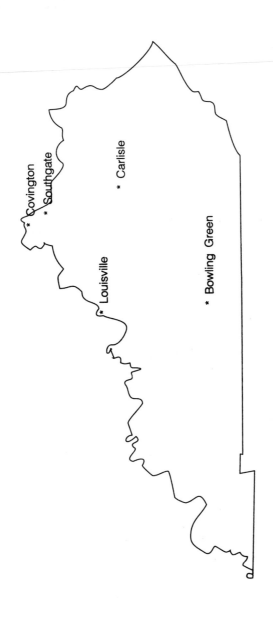

BOWLING GREEN

288. Shrine of Mary, Mother of the Church & Model of All Christians, St. Joseph Church

The small chapel attached to the rectory of the old and beautiful church was designated a diocesan shrine in May 1989 by the Bishop of Owensboro. There are weekly holy hours, an annual Marian Congress and a Eucharistic Retreat and other special events.

Mailing address: Marian Shrine Committee, 434 Church Street, Bowling Green, KY

(9:00 a.m. to 5:00 p.m.)

CARLISLE

289. Shrine of Our Lady of Guadalupe, 617 East Main Street

Originally known as St. John Church, the shrine was established in 1962 by Bishop Richard H. Ackerman of Covington to serve as the Marian shrine of his diocese. A tapestry of Our Lady of Guadalupe hangs above the altar.

(Always open)

COVINGTON

290. Shrine of St. Ann, St. Ann Church, 1274 Parkway

The practice of holding an annual Solemn Novena in honor of the mother of the Blessed Virgin is now 100-years-old. Beginning on July 18, the devotion culminates on July 26 (the feast of St. Ann) with a candle-light procession. Fr. Louis G. Clermont, a French Canadian, established the shrine in 1888 and obtained the two relics enshrined there. The first is a fragment of rock from St. Ann's room in Jerusalem. And the second is a portion of her finger bone.

(Open during services only)

LOUISVILLE

291. Lourdes Rosary Shrine, St. Louis Bertrand Church, 1104 South 6th Street

Twenty-six years after the apparition of the Immaculate Conception to St. Bernadette in France, the Dominicans constructed a replica of the famous grotto at the request of the parishioners. The shrine is located in a recess near the sanctuary on the left side of the church. Five steps lead down to it, giving it a cave-like appearance. Inside is a grotto with statues of Our Lady and St. Bernadette. Since 1884 many favors — both spiritual and material — have been granted. At each of the three Solemn Novenas held each year, thousands of petitions arrive by mail from all over the country. *(7:00 a.m. to 7:00 p.m.)*

SOUTHGATE

292. *Shrine of the Little Flower, St. Therese Church, Alexandria Pike*

Though the parish was established in 1927, the current church dates from 1964. Since its beginning, the church has been recognized as a diocesan shrine. A statue of the Little Flower stands outside the church and another occupies a prominent place within. The shrine possesses three first-class relics of St. Therese obtained from Mother Agnes de Jesus, the surviving sister of the Saint and prioress of the Community of Mt. Carmel at Lisieux, France. There is a weekly novena to the Little Flower.
(Open during services only)

LOUISIANA

CAMERON

293. Shrine to the Mother of God, Protectress from Storms, Louisiana Highway 27

When Hurricane Audrey struck the coast of Louisiana, 500 people were killed and millions of dollars of property damage resulted. Following the 1957 disaster, an inquiry was made regarding what could be done to prevent a recurrence. Bishop Maurice Schexnayder of Lafayette suggested they "erect a beautiful, lasting monument to the Mother of God, which would serve as a perpetual entreaty to her Son, the Master of the Universe, to protect Cameron parish and the surrounding area from future calamities." Dedicated in 1963, the 36-foot shrine shelters a 7-foot marble statue of Our Lady and the young Jesus standing on a pedestal. An inscription reads "Do not harm my children."

Mailing address: Our Lady, Star of the Sea Church, Cameron, LA

CONVENT

294. St. Michael the Archangel Church

Directly behind the main altar of this Marist staffed church is the Our Lady of Lourdes Chapel. Dedicated in 1876, the grotto was constructed out of sugar cane clinkers by two parishioners: Christopher Columbe and Florian Dicharry. Built eighteen years after the Blessed Virgin's apparition to Bernadette Soubirous and two years before her death, it is considered by many to be the first Lourdes shrine in the United States.
(6:30 a.m. to 6:30 p.m.)

DURALDE

295. Sacred Heart Shrine

On July 20, 1982 while on retreat at Grand Coteau, Fr. Edward Fontaine received in a dream what he considered to be a commission to build a shrine in honor of the Sacred Heart. As he set to work, obstacles quickly vanished and the money poured in; by the end of the following year the shrine had been completed and dedicated by Bishop Frey of Lafayette. The chapel's most celebrated feature is its stained glass windows, thirteen of which are said to be at least 200 years old and priceless. Each year on the Feast of the Sacred Heart (June 21) or on the Sunday after, pilgrims flock to the Duralde shrine. On the first Monday of each month Charismatics from five parishes meet here. Many favors have been granted: healings, conversions, etc.

Mailing address: Eunice, LA
(Always open)

GRAND COTEAU

296. Shrine of St. John Berchmans, Academy of the Sacred Heart, 1821 Academy Road

Two saints and a candidate for canonization are associated with this school and convent. The first is St. Philippine Duchesne who was instrumental in establishing the convent and who visited here twice. Then there is Mother Cornelia Connelly, foundress of the Sisters of the Holy Family and candidate for sainthood, who taught here. The last is St. John Berchmans whose apparitions here are the chief cause of Grand Coteau's fame. The 17th century Belgian Jesuit saint was only twenty-two when he died but during his brief life he impressed all by his humility, piety and his strict observance of the Rule of the Society of Jesus. He is the patron of seminarians and sodalists. When the sisters of the convent prayed a novena to the then uncanonized saint in 1866, the gravely-ill Mary Wilson was miraculously cured of her afflictions. The beneficiary of the favor reported that the young Jesuit had appeared to her and assured that her suffering was over. Rome accepted the miracle as authentic and it led to the canonization of St. John Berchmans. The shrine is on the second floor of the academy in the room in which the apparition took place.
(10:00 a.m to 4:00 p.m. M-F; 1:00 p.m. to 4:00 p.m. Sat. and Sun.)

NEW ORLEANS

297. St. Ann National Shrine, 2101 Ursuline Ave.

Devotion to the grandmother of Jesus has been part of the life of this parish since its beginning in 1852. But it was not until fifty years later, with the arrival of Fr. John Baptist Bogaertts, that the beautiful shrine to St. Ann was established and a confraternity founded. Since then solemn novenas and other special devotions in her honor have been popular. In 1920, the church and shrine were moved to their present location. Six years later, Pope Pius XI recognized it as a national shrine. It is said that over 70,000 petitions arrive by mail each year. In addition to the shrine in the church, there is also an outdoor sanctuary. Entering from Ursuline Avenue one first encounters a grotto containing an altar and statue of St. Ann with the Blessed Virgin; above, in a niche stands the image of the Immaculate Conception, as at Lourdes. Nearby is a reproduction of the Scala Sancta (Holy Stairway) of the Church of San Salvatore in Rome.

Mailing address: 4920 Lovelend Street, Metairie, LA
(8:00 a.m. to 3:30 p.m. M-S; 8:00 a.m. to 11:45 a.m. Sun.)

298. International Shrine of St. Jude, Our Lady of Guadalupe Church, 411 North Rampart Street

Originally known as the "Mortuary Chapel" because of its origins during the Yellow Fever plague of 1826, Our Lady of Guadalupe is the oldest surviving church in the New Orleans area. Fr. Turgis, the famous Civil War chaplain, renovated it in the postbellum period. In the 1880s the church served Italian immigrants who had flocked to the city. By the turn of the century, however, Our Lady of Guadalupe had become a religious center for the Spanish-speaking. Under the administration of the Oblates of Mary Immaculate, the church has developed into a shrine to St. Jude. Services in honor of the Saint of Miracles are broadcast on ten radio stations each Sunday and Solemn Novenas are held in the months of January, July and October. A statue of St. Jude facing Rampart Street stands between twin fountains. Inside, there are mosaics and murals by Charles Reineke.
(7:00 a.m. to 6:30 p.m.)

299. The National Votive Shrine of Our Lady of Prompt Succor, Ursuline Convent Chapel, 2635 State Street

When Mother St. Michael asked permission to join her fellow Ursuline Sisters in Louisiana, the Bishop of Montpelier refused to let her go. Mother St. Michael then wrote to the Pope. When doing so, she promised the Blessed Virgin that if she received a prompt and favorable answer she would popularize Our Lady of Prompt Succor

in the New World. Her request was granted. On New Year's Day, 1810, Mother St. Michael arrived in New Orleans with her hand carved statue of Our Lady of Prompt Succor. This image she installed in the Ursuline Convent chapel. Five years later, when the British were advancing on New Orleans, the women of the city thronged the sisters' chapel beseaching the Blessed Virgin's intercession. Their prayers were answered by General Andrew Jackson's victory. Devotion to the Our Lady of Prompt Succor spread rapidly. In 1851, Pope Pius IX gave formal approval for the celebration of the Feast of Our Lady of Prompt Succor each January 15. Forty-three years later, the statue was solemnly crowned with the consent of the Pope. By 1924, the sisters had moved to State Street and the new National Shrine was dedicated. (In the Gothic chapel on the grounds of the Ursuline Convent, Mother St. Michael's Madonna is enthroned under a stone canopy.) In 1928, Our Lady of Prompt Succor was declared patroness of New Orleans and of the state of Louisiana.
(Open during services and by appointment)

300. National Shrine of St. Roch, Chapel of St. Roch Cemetery, 1725 St. Roch Avenue

During the epidemic of Yellow Fever in 1868, the parishioners of Holy Trinity Church led by Fr. Peter Leonard Trevis turned to St. Roch. Their prayers were answered: not a single parishioner was struck down. In gratitude a shrine to the saint was established in 1875. The path leading to the small Gothic chapel is now paved with stones marking favors received and the walls are covered with votive offerings. Above the altar is a statue of St. Roch; four side panels depict scenes from his life. Fr. Trevis is buried there. Three times a year pilgrims inundate the little chapel whose seating capacity is sixty. On St. Roch's Day (August 16), All Saint's Day and Good Friday large numbers of worshipers come to participate in traditional services. It is believed by many that if a young woman visits here daily for nine days and invokes the saint's intercession, she will find a good husband.
(8:00 a.m. to 4:00 p.m. M-Sat.)

301. Father Seelos Center, St. Mary's Assumption Church, 2030 Constance Street

Born in Fussen, Germany, Francis Seelos showed an interest in becoming a priest while still quite young. In 1843 he came to America, joined the Redemptorists and was ordained the following year. In Pittsburgh, he worked for several years under St. John Neumann at St. Philomena Church. In subsequent years, he served as pastor, novice master, seminary director and parish mission preacher. In 1860 he declined the honor of being chosen Bishop of Pittsburgh. Always known for his personal piety, he was noted for his ability to bring peace to troubled souls in the confessional. Moreover, many over whom he prayed were cured of their physical ailments. Father Seelos died in New Orleans in 1867 after contracting Yellow Fever. He is buried in this German Baroque style church where he had served as pastor for two years prior to his death. Weekly prayer services are held for his canonization.

(Open during services only)

MARYLAND

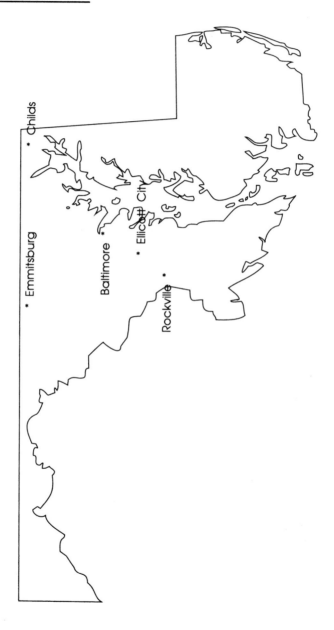

BALTIMORE

302. Mother Seton House on Paca Street, 600 North Paca Street

For approximately one year, this Federal period house served as a home for America's first native born saint and her family. While occupying the premises, Elizabeth Ann Seton conducted a school for girls including her own three daughters. And in March 1809 she took her first vows as a religious in the presence of Archbishop John Carroll at nearby St. Mary's Seminary Chapel. Thereafter, she was known as Mother Seton. In June of the same year, the saint moved to Emmitsburg, Maryland. The house has been restored and furnished with period furniture. Operated by the Sulpician Fathers, the Seton home is open to visitors on Saturday and Sunday.
(1:00 p.m. to 4:00 p.m.)

303. St. Jude Shrine, St. John the Baptist Church, 308 North Paca Street

Administered by the Pallottine Fathers of the Immaculate Conception Province, the church has become a nationwide center for devotions to the Patron Saint of Difficult Cases. Located in downtown Baltimore, St. John Church was built in 1873 and intended to serve as a national parish for Italian immigrants. Shortly after the outbreak of World War II, novenas in honor of St. Jude began. They proved popular and by 1953, the shrine was established. Thousands of people from all over the United States and Canada visit each year and even more keep in touch by mail. Perpetual novena services are held four times a day each Wednesday.
(Open during services only)

CHILDS

304. The Shrine of Our Lady of the Highways

On a foggy night in October 1968, nineteen cars piled up in a tragic accident near the novitiate of the Oblates of St. Francis de Sales. Four years later, unable to get the tragedy out of his mind, Fr. John Fuqua built this shrine on a hill overlooking the John F. Kennedy Expressway (I-95). It is intended to serve as a memorial to those who died there and as a "prayer in stone" for all who drive the nation's highways. He also founded the Spiritual Travelers, a religious society devoted to highway safety. On all national holidays, Masses are offered for travelers.

ELLICOTT CITY

305. Our Lady's Center, 3301 South Rogers Avenue

People from all parts of the Baltimore metropolitan area visit this lay-operated oratory and retreat center dedicated to the Blessed Virgin. Its focal points are the Chapel of the Annunciation and the Shrine Room of Our Lady of Fatima, the home of the Maryland Pilgrim Virgin statue. Also on the grounds is Our Lady's Grove, site of the outdoor Stations of the Cross.

(9:00 a.m. to 5:00 p.m. M-F; 12:00 p.m. to 2:00 p.m. Sat. and Sun.)

EMMITSBURG

306. National Shrine Grotto of Lourdes, Mount St. Mary's College

It was Fr. John Dubois, French Sulpician and founder of the famous college and seminary who first discovered the natural grotto and erected a cross sometime before 1815. Later, a statue of Mary would be placed here also. St. Elizabeth Seton often visited the spot in the early days. Fr. Gabriel Brute, her spiritual director, did much to expand and improve the grotto. By the 1830s the custom of holding Corpus Christi processions had already begun. In 1875 a seminarian, having read of Our Lady's apparition to St. Bernadette, suggested the grotto as an excellent locale in which to build a shrine to Our Lady of Lourdes. Fr. John A. Waterson, president of the college, heartily approved and the project was swiftly completed. The new shrine gradually replaced the old. (A memorial chapel, built in 1906 now marks the location of the original grotto.) Though the Lourdes shrine's fame was for a long time mainly local, by the 1950s the number of pilgrims had greatly increased. Under the direction of Monsignor Hugh Philips, the Marian sanctuary has been greatly enhanced. A crucifixion group now overlooks the 900 seat outdoor amphitheater and grotto. Station of the Cross and a Rosary Lane have been added and a 125-foot Marian Campanile stands at the entrance. Other additions are Our Lady of the Lake, shrines to St.

Francis and Mother Seton and the restored Corpus Christi chapel.
Novenas to Our Lady of Lourdes are held regularly.

307. National Shrine of St. Elizabeth Ann Seton, St. Joseph's Provincial House of the Daughters of Charity, 333 South Seton Avenue

After leaving her house on Paca Street in Baltimore, Mother Seton
and her small band of followers moved to Emmitsburg where they lived
first at the Stone House and a year later, at the White House. Here she
established St. Joseph's Academy, the first parochial school in America.
In 1812, the rule of her fledgling community was approved by Bishop
Carroll of Baltimore. The following year, she and eighteen other sisters
took their permanent vows. Thus the Sisters of Charity, the first
American Religious society was founded. The order spread rapidly and
by the time of Mother Seton's death in 1821, it numbered twenty
communities. Visitors to the shrine may visit the Stone House, which
has been restored, the White House where she died and the Mortuary
Chapel where her remains reposed between 1846 and 1968. Her final
resting place is in the Seton Shrine Chapel. Canonized in 1975 by Pope
Paul VI, Mother Seton is the first American-born saint.

On August 4, 1991, the shrine was dedicated as a basilica. Only
35 churches in the United States have received this papal designation
which is bestowed upon churches which are outstanding in antiquity,
dignity, historical importance or significance as a center of devotion
and worship.
(10:00 a.m. to 5:00 p.m.)

ROCKVILLE

308. Shrine of St. Jude, 12701 Veirs Mill Road

There is an annual novena to the Patron Saint of the Impossible in
October.
*(6:30 a.m. to 6:00 p.m. M-F; 7:00 a.m. to 8:00 p.m. Sat.; 7:30 a.m.
to 7:00 p.m. Sun.)*

MISSOURI

CARTHAGE

309. Immaculate Heart of Mary Shrine, 1900 Grand Avenue

The Congregation of The Mother CoRedemptrix (CMC) was founded in Vietnam in 1953 by Dominic Mary Tran Dinh-Thu to evangelize non-Catholics and to promote devotion to the Blessed Virgin Mary. Twenty-two years later, following the fall of Saigon, many of the CoRedemptrix priests and brothers fled to America where they were welcomed by Bishop Bernard F. Law of Springfield-Cape Girardeau, Missouri. The order now serves Indo-Chinese refugees in more than a dozen U.S. dioceses and operates the only all-Vietnamese seminary in the country. The CoRedemptrix Fathers also staff the Immaculate Heart of Mary Shrine. A 33-foot concrete statue of the Blessed Mother and Child rescuing a man dominates the shrine's Our Lady of Peace Square. The refugee order hosts a Marian Day each August.
(7:00 a.m. to 10:00 p.m.)

EUREKA

310. Black Madonna Shrine and Grottos

Operated by the Franciscan Missionary Brothers of the Sacred Heart of Jesus, the U.S. branch of which he founded, the Eureka sanctuary is the work of one man: Bro. Bronislaus Luszcz. Beginning in 1938, the Polish-born shrine builder spent the last twenty-two years of his life constructing these grottos. Started as a simple tribute to Our Lady of Czestochowa (the Black Madonna), it developed into a shrine complex including eight grottos, the Way of the Cross, the Franciscan Seven Joys Rosary Stations and an open-air chapel honoring the Polish Virgin. Constructed of Missouri Barite rock, the grottos honor Our Lady of Perpetual Help, St. Joseph, the Agony in the Garden, St. Francis, the Nativity, the Assumption and Coronation of the Blessed Mother, and Our Lady of Sorrows.
(8:00 a.m. until dark)

PERRYVILLE

311. National Shrine of Our Lady of the Miraculous Medal, St. Mary of The Barrens Church, St. Joseph Street

The design of the Sacred Medal of the Blessed and Immaculate Virgin Mary, as it is officially known, was revealed by the Mother of God to St. Catherine Laboure in 1830. Seven years later the present church staffed by Vincentian priests from the adjacent St. Mary Seminary was dedicated. The original humble shrine to Our Lady of the Miraculous Medal in the transept of the old Renaissance Church, was replaced by the present ornate Marian sanctuary on the 100th anniversary of the Rue du Bac apparitions. On the richly ornamented shrine altar of white marble stands a statue of the Our Lady of Grace type. Among the other notable features of the church are its tall bell tower and the stained glass windows which tell the story of the Immaculata's appearance to Sister Catherine. The magnificent main altar displays an attractive representation of Our Lady's Assumption. Nearby is the restored 1818 log house of worship, the predecessor of St. Mary of the Barrens. Beyond, on a wooded mound, stands the statue of Our Lady of St. Mary's. From there a path leads to a grotto in honor of Our Lady of the Miraculous Medal built by the seminarians during World War I. Novenas are held at the shrine every Monday morning.
(Always open)

PORTAGE DES SIOUX

312. Our Lady of the River Shrine

The twenty-seven foot, 3,000-pound statue stands near the confluence of the Mississippi, Missouri and Illinois Rivers. Six hundred feet off the shore of Portage, it is the site of the annual blessing of the fleet. At night, the lighted statue is a navigation aid and is officially recognized as such by the U.S. Coast Guard. Erected in 1957, under the leadership of Father Edward B. Schlattman, the shrine is an expression of gratitude by the people of Portage for having been spared from flooding several years earlier.

Mailing address: c/o St. Francis Church, Portage des Sioux, MO

ST. CHARLES

313. St. Philippine Duchesne Shrine, Sacred Heart Academy, 619 South Second Street

The foundress of the American branch of the Society of the Sacred Heart arrived from France in 1818. Settling first at St. Charles, she established the first free school west of the Mississippi. Moving to Florissant, Missouri she proceeded to build a school, convent and a novitiate for her growing religious community. From here foundations were made in Louisiana and St. Louis. In 1841, at the invitation of Father Pierre De Smet, she came to Sugar Creek, Kansas to serve the Potawatomi Indians. Unfortunately, her health failed her and she was unable to learn the language. But the Indians loved her; they called her "the women who always prays." Two years later she returned to St. Charles where she died in 1852. The sisters have built a memorial chapel here to house her remains and her room has been preserved. St. Philippine Duchesne was canonized July 3, 1988.

(9:00 a.m. to 11:00 a.m. and 1:00 p.m. to 3:00 p.m. Tue., Thur., Fri.; 10:00 a.m. to 12:00 p.m. and 1:00 p.m. to 3:00 p.m. Sat.; 12:00 p.m. to 3:00 p.m. Sun.; closed Mon. and Wed.)

ST. LOUIS

314. Shrine of Our Lady of Perpetual Help, St. Alphonsus Rock Church, Church, 1118 North Grand Boulevard

Called the "Rock" Church because of the large amount of stone used in its construction, veneration to Our Lady of Perpetual Help has been prominent here since the beginning. The popularity of devotions in her honor peaked during the Great Depression when as many as 18,000 people came here on Tuesdays. The present shrine, located near the sanctuary, was blessed in 1922. Here the painting of the Redemptorist Madonna is enshrined on a "lancet gothic" style altar. Among the interesting features of the church are its 237-foot steeple; its great bells, one of which weighs five tons and its impressive main altar. Novenas are still held three times daily on Tuesday.

(Open during services only)

315. Mt. Grace Convent, 1438 East Warne Avenue

The Sister Servants of the Holy Spirit are a cloistered community of nuns devoted to perpetual adoration. Their hill top chapel was dedicated in 1928 and is open to the public. Here the "Pink Sisters," as they are known, take their turn throughout the day and night adoring the Blessed Sacrament. Part of the fame of the Convent results from the existence of the Legion of One Thousand Men. Begun in 1958 at the urging of Cardinal Ritter, the sole obligation of its members is a weekly visit to the Blessed Sacrament exposed at Mt. Grace or at some other place having perpetual adoration. (There are two other such sites in St. Louis.)

(5:15 a.m. to 8:15 p.m. M-F; 7:30 a.m. to 8:15 p.m. Sun.)

316. Shrine of St. Joseph, 1220 North Eleventh Street

Built in 1844 and once the largest parish in St. Louis, the shrine has the distinction of being the locale of two miracles. Twenty years after the church's founding, the wife of Ignatius Streker, hearing a sermon on the intercessory powers of Blessed Peter Claver, rushed home to her gravely ill husband. At her urging the German immigrant came to the church, was blessed with the relic of the saint and within a week, the man whose doctor had given him two weeks to live was completely well. (The cure was later accepted by the Vatican as one of the miracles necessary for the canonization of the 17th century Jesuit.) In 1866, when Asiatic Cholera was taking 200 lives a day in St. Louis, at the suggestion of Fr. Joseph Weber, the parishioners promised St. Joseph that if they were spared, they would build a suitable monument to him. Their prays were answered: from that day on, not a single member of the church was stricken. In thanksgiving, the Altar of Answered Prayers was erected at the church. The monument is a replica of the Altar of St. Ignatius in the Jesuit Gesu Church in Rome, except that the figures of St. Joseph and the Child Jesus were substituted for St. Ignatius. Beneath them are the words "Ite ad Joseph" — Go to Joseph. Noted for its architecture as well as its miracles, the shrine is listed in the National Register of Historic Places. Masses is celebrated each Sunday at 11:00 a.m. On St. Joseph's Day, blessed bread and fruit are distributed.

(Open during services only)

ST. PATRICK

317. Shrine of St. Patrick

Being the only town in the world with a post office bearing the name of Ireland's patron saint, St. Patrick, Missouri seemed an appropriate site at which to build a shrine to the Shamrock Saint. That is what Fr. Francis O'Duignan, himself born in Eire (Ireland), thought when he arrived here. It took him twenty-two years, but in 1957 he finally realized his dream. The Shrine of St. Patrick is Gaelic in design, being modeled after the Church of Four Masters near Donegal, Ireland. Outside stands a large statue of the saint and another can be found within. The church has thirty-six stained glass windows imported from Ireland showing illustrations from the Book of Kells. The Rose Windows features a portrait of the saint surrounded by the symbols of the Emerald Isle's provinces. There is an annual celebration on March 17, St. Patrick's Day.
(Open during services and by appointment)

ST. PETER

318. Our Lady of the Way Shrine, Sue Mandy Drive

Formerly located near the junction of 1-70 and Route 79, the shrine was constructed in 1955-6 at the suggestion of Msgr. Anthony Strauss. The Marian sanctuary is still maintained by a group of dedicated laymen. Threatened with destruction to make way for a cloverleaf interchange, it was moved to its present location two miles east and rededicated in 1987. The Shrine consists of a 6-foot statue of the Blessed Virgin holding the child Jesus. The sculpture stands in the central alcove of a brick wall-like structure beside a pond.

STARKENBURG

319. Shrine of Our Lady of Sorrows, St. Martin Church

The first church at the site was built of logs but it had in its possession the "White Lady," a statue of the Mother of God which the villagers often carried in procession. After a new stone house of worship was constructed in 1873, a larger statue was placed within, the old Madonna being relegated to the attic of a monastery. There it stayed for many years until August Mitsch, the new sacristan of St. Martin discovered it. He built a small chapel for it on the church grounds and before long pious parishioners began to visit it. However, as the fame of the little shrine in the woods increased, a Marian statue of the "Pieta of Achtermann" type was installed and the "White Lady" again banished to an attic. Yet blessings were showered on the parish. In 1891, the village crops were saved when they turned to Our Lady of Sorrows for help. Three years later, the Pieta emerged miraculously unharmed from a fire and the parishioners faith in Our Sorrowful Mother brought an end to a drought. As the Starkenburg shrine's fame spread, pilgrims came from St. Louis and surrounding states. In 1897, Pope Leo XIII granted an indulgence to those visiting the Marian sanctuary. Two years later the Confraternity of the Seven Dolors was established here. The following year the Lourdes Grotto was constructed and a new Way of the Cross built. In 1910, Archbishop John Glennon dedicated a beautiful new stone Romanesque church. The repaired and repainted "White Lady" now stands on the main altar and Our Lady of Sorrow has her own side chapel whose walls are lined with tokens acknowledging favors granted. Among the other attractions of the shrine are the Mount of Olives Grotto and the Mount Calvary scene located above the underground sepulchre. Public pilgrimages are held on the third Sunday of May and the Second Sunday of September.

Mailing address: c/o Church of the Risen Savior, Rhineland, MO *(8:30 a.m. until sunset)*

MISSISSIPPI

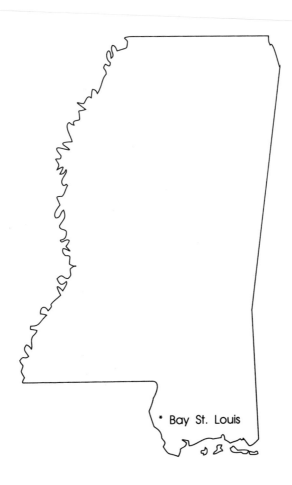

* Bay St. Louis

BAY ST. LOUIS

320. St. Augustine Seminary, Ulman Avenue

Founded in 1923, this historic site operated by the Divine Word Fathers, was the first U.S. Catholic seminary to admit African-American candidates for the priesthood. Six Black bishops are among its alumni. On the grounds are two shrines: a highway Sacred Heart shrine, the second of its kind in the United States, and an Agony Grotto. The latter contains five statues, namely the Agony in the Garden, Christ in Prison, the Pieta, Jesus in the Tomb and a Resurrection motif.

MONTANA

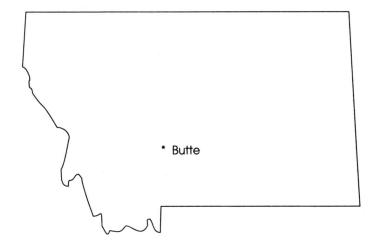

* Butte

BUTTE

321. Our Lady of the Rockies

On a mountain overlooking the city stands a 90-foot white metal statue of the Blessed Mother put there by helicopter in December, 1985. Originally conceived by Bob O'Bill as a thanksgiving offering after his wife's recovery from a dangerous surgery, the project took six years to complete. Lighted at night, the 51-ton Marian monument atop Saddle Rock, 8,500 feet above sea level, is a spectacular sight. The madonna has drawn visitors from all over the United States and from seventeen foreign countries. A hilltop chapel and aerial lift to the statue are planned.

Mailing address: Our Lady of the Rockies Foundation, P.O. Box 4050, Butte, MT

NEVADA

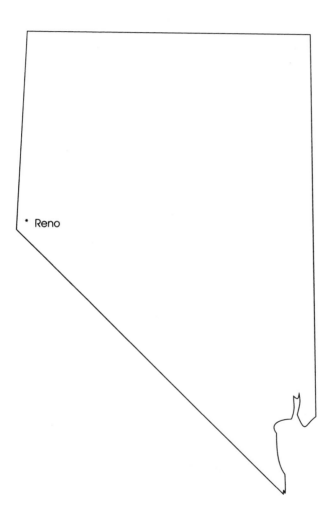

* Reno

RENO

322. St. Therese — Little Flower Catholic Church, 875 East Plumb Lane

Modernistic in design, the church is famous for its devotions to St. Jude. Novenas to the Patron Saint of Difficult Cases are on Tuesdays after the 12:00 p.m. and 7:00 p.m. Masses. The church is open every day from 6:00 in the morning until midnight.

NEW MEXICO

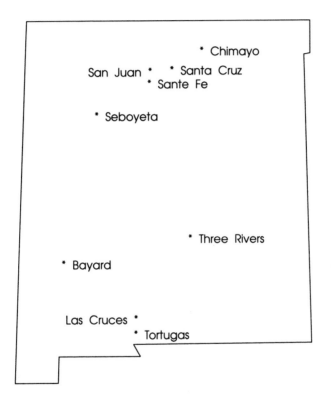

* Chimayo

San Juan *   * Santa Cruz
             * Sante Fe

* Seboyeta

* Three Rivers

* Bayard

Las Cruces *
           * Tortugas

BAYARD

323. Shrine of Our Lady of Guadalupe, Our Lady of Fatima Church

The shrine and the nearby church are under the care of the Augustinian Recollect Fathers. Dedicated in 1962, the Marian sanctuary consists of a Way of the Cross which leads up a hill, at the summit of which is a cross and monument to Our Lady of Guadalupe. On Good Friday, pilgrims climb the mount, stopping to pray at each station. And on December 12, the Virgin is serenaded with the *mananitas* at 5:00 in the morning.

CHIMAYO

324.The Shrine of Our Lord of Esquipulas

On the west slope of the Sangre de Cristo Mountains, near the headwaters of Santa Cruz River stands the village of Chimayo, site of one of the Southwest's most famous shrines. Built in 1816 by Don Bernardo Abeyta, the Santuario is dedicated to Our Lord of Esquipulas — a devotion originating in Guatamala in the late 16th century, centering on a famous crucifix. Owned by the Abeyta family for several generations, the shrine was acquired by the Archdiocese of Santa Fe in 1929 and placed under the care of the priests of the Congregation of the Sons of the Holy Family. The twin-towered adobe church built in the Spanish colonial style was designated a National Historical Landmark in 1970. The most prominent feature of the interior is its five beautiful reredos (series of sacred paintings): one behind the main altar and two on each side of the nave. Of particular significance to the people of Chimayo is the *bultos* (carving) of St. James. Devotion to "El Senor Santiago" is also reflected in the annual "Moros y Christianos" pageant commemorating the battle of Clavijo (Spain) in which the saint is said to have taken a leading part. Called the "Lourdes of America," the Santuario is famous for the many healings, both spiritual and physical which have taken place there. It is the custom for those who are ill to take some of the earth from the "pozito" to use as medicine, a small amount at a time taken with a glass of water.
(9:00 a.m. to 6:00 p.m. Summer; 9:00 a.m. to 4:30 p.m. Winter)

LAS CRUCES

325. Our Lady of Health Church, 1178 North Mesquite

As a result of the Blessed Virgin's intercession during the epidemic of 1752 *La Santisima Virgen de la Salud* is the patroness of the region of Rotova, Valencia. It was Fr. Jose G. Saez who brought devotion to Our Lady of Health from his native Spain to this border town. Established in 1955, the church possesses a beautiful imported replica of the Rotova Madonna.
(Open during services only)

SAN JUAN PUEBLO

326. Our Lady of Lourdes Pilgrimage Shrine

The first permanent Spanish settlement in New Mexico was established at San Juan in 1598. Later in the same year a mission chapel was built, remaining in use for forty-five years. It was replaced first by another chapel and then by a much larger church which served for almost 200 years until it was torn down to make room for the present parish church. In 1888 on the 30th anniversary of the apparitions to St. Bernadette, Fr. Camillus Seux imported a huge statue of the Immaculata from France. This he placed on a pedestal in front of the San Juan Church. The following year, he began work on the Gothic style shrine to Our Lady of Lourdes which can still be seen today.
(Open during services only)

SANTA CRUZ

327. Holy Cross Church

Served by the Sons of Holy Family, this is the second oldest parish in New Mexico. The church has in its possession a statue of *Jesus Nazareno* to which the Hermanos Penitentes have a special devotion. Carved in the mid 1800s, the Santo is carried in procession on Good Friday. Old legends attribute miraculous powers to it. On one occasion, Jesus Nazareno is said to have stopped a flood and on another, to have halted an epidemic.
(9:00 a.m. to 12:00 p.m. and 1:00 p.m. to 4:00 p.m. M-F; 7:00 a.m. to 2:00 p.m. Sun.)

SANTA FE

328. Loretto Chapel, 219 College Street

Twenty-one years after their arrival in Santa Fe, the Sisters of Loretto decided to build their own chapel. At the insistence of Bishop Lamy, it was patterned after the famous *Sainte-Chapelle* in Paris, France. Begun in 1873, it was finished five years later. As the structure was nearing completion, it was noted that though the chapel had a choir loft, there were no stairs leading up to it. Several builders were consulted but each said that because of the height of the loft, stairs would take up too much room to be practical. At this point the sisters began a novena to St. Joseph. On the ninth day, an elderly carpenter arrived and offered his services free. He set to work immediately using only a saw, a T-square and a hammer. When the work was completed he could not be found. When the Sisters tried to locate him, it was discovered that he had not purchased anything from the local lumber yard. To make the matter even more mysterious, experts say the wood used was not native to New Mexico. Some say it came from the Holy Land — and that the old man was St. Joseph himself. And the stairway itself is a mystery — and an architectural wonder. Consisting of thirty-three stairs, it makes two complete 360-degree turns. Yet there are no nails nor central support to give it stability. Some architects have stated that it should have collapsed the first day — but though it was in continuous use for eighty-five years, it never did. The chapel is now privately owned but it is still open to the public.
(9:00 a.m. to 5:00 p.m.)

329. Cathedral of St. Francis of Assisi, Cathedral Plaza

Enshrined in the Lady Chapel of the Cathedral is a small wooden statue of the Blessed Virgin brought to Santa Fe by Fray Alonso Benavides in 1625. Immediately, "La Conquistadora" — as she was known — won the hearts of the Spaniards and Indians alike. When the Pueblo Indians revolted fifty-five years later, the Spanish colonists fled, taking the Marian image with them to Mexico. On their return in 1693, their leader, Don Diego de Vargas, vowed that if the city was retaken, he would once more return the beloved statue to the Santa Fe mission church — now the Cathedral of St. Francis —

and institute an annual celebration in her honor. In 1807, the Rosario Chapel was built at the site where Vargas made his promise. It is to this sanctuary on the outskirts of town that "La Conquistadora" is taken in solemn procession each year. There follows a week of religious festivities. The following Sunday, the guard of honor, the "Caballeros de Vargas" return the Virgin to her ornate shrine in the Cathedral. In 1960, "La Conquistadora" was given the honor of a papal coronation and received a crown of gold, silver and precious stones. The Cathedral of St. Francis of Assisi, the sixth church at that site, was dedicated in 1886 by Most Rev. John Baptist Lamy, first American bishop of Santa Fe. The church was renovated in 1966 and again twenty years later, with the approach of the centenary of the first blessing of the church. The doors of the cathedral's main entrance, incorporate sixteen bronze panels depicting the religious history of New Mexico. A San Damiano Cross dominates the interior above the sanctuary. Behind the main altar is a Reredos showing the more outstanding saints of the Americans.
(6:00 a.m. to 6:00 p.m. M-S; 6:00 a.m. to 7:00 p.m. Sun.)

SEBOYETA

330. Shrine of Our Lady of Lourdes
Founded in the mid-18th century by Spanish settlers, Seboyeta is dominated by Our Lady of Sorrows Church. Built in 1823, it replaces an earlier Franciscan mission. North of town there is a natural grotto with a spring where the Spanish colonists built a shrine to Our Lady of Mercy. However, since the 19th century, the site has become a sanctuary dedicated to Our Lady of Lourdes.

Mailing address: c/o Our Lady of Sorrows Church, Seboyeta, NM

THREE RIVERS

331. Santo Nino de Atocha Shrine
An old Spanish legend says that three or four hundred years ago, the child Jesus visited the Village of Atocha, Spain. Dressed as a typical shepard boy with sun hat, staff and gourd for water, he was welcomed and fed. After his departure, his true identity was revealed when a series of miracles took place in the village church before a

statue depicting him as he looked when he visited them. The devotion to the *Santo Nino* (Holy Child) spread to Mexico and from there to this country. Built by Senator Albert B. Fall in 1916, the shrine was restored ten years later by Fr. Bonaventure Nava, OFM. Overlooking the church is a mountain called *El Cerro del Nino*, on whose summit stands a 20-foot cross placed there in 1964. Six years later, Stations of the Cross were erected along the path leading up the 3,000 foot slope to *La Cruz de Santo Nino de Atocha*.

Mailing address: c/o St. Francis de Paula Church, Tularosa, NM
(Always open)

TORTUGAS

332. Shrine and Parish of Our Lady of Guadalupe

When the Spaniards were driven out of northern New Mexico during the 17th century Pueblo Revolt, many Christian Indians fled also. Some of the refugees settled in this village, a few miles south of Las Cruces, near the Rio Grande. Later when they were faced with another danger, the Indians prayed to Our Lady of Guadalupe for protection. To commemorate their having been spared, the Tortugans hold an annual celebration each December 10th through 12th. After prayer and dancing in honor of the Blessed Virgin, a pilgrimage is made to the top of the nearby mountain. A day of prayer and fasting follows, climaxing with Masses. At sunset they descend, lighting bonfires along their path, thus illuminating the mountain. Afterwards there is a fiesta.

Mailing address: Mesilla Park, NM
(8:00 a.m. to 6:30 p.m. M-F; 7:30 a.m. to 6:30 p.m. Sun.)

NORTH CAROLINA

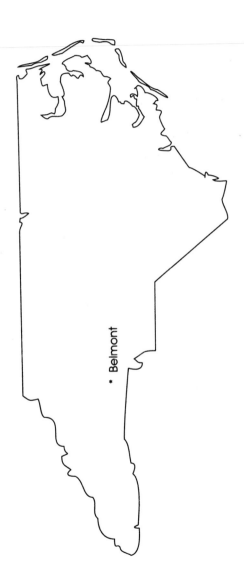

* Belmont

BELMONT

333. Shrine of Our Lady of Lourdes, Belmont Abbey

When one of the monks was cured of Typhoid Fever through the intercession of Our Lady of Lourdes, a grotto honoring her was built in thanksgiving. Dedicated in 1891, *Maria Lourdes* as it is known is the only pilgrimage shrine in the state. The Marian sanctuary is open to visitors throughout the year and during May, the Benedictines conduct nightly devotions. Nearby there is a small shrine — consisting of a statue, fountain and gazebo — dedicated to St. Walburga.

OKLAHOMA

* Bison

Oklahoma City * * Prague

BISON

334. Our Lady of Fatima Shrine, St. Joseph Church

Begun by Fr. Andrew Thomas and completed by Fr. John O'Brien, the Marian sanctuary was dedicated in 1951. The official Fatima shrine of the diocese of Oklahoma City is located on the grounds of St. Joseph Church. There is a perpetual novena to the Portugese Madonna every Wednesday evening. Each year, nine days of devotion to Our Lady of Fatima are held May 4 to 13 and October 4 to 13 inclusive.

OKLAHOMA CITY

335. Our Lady of Mt. Carmel and St. Therese Little Flower Catholic Church, 1125 South Walker Street

Famous for its campanile which is visible from most parts of the city, the church adjoins the monastery and headquarters of the St. Therese of Oklahoma Province of the Discalced Carmelites. In 1920, the first statue of the Saint of the Little Way to be venerated in the United States was installed in the original shrine. To accommodate increased attendance, the present church was built in 1927. Two of its outstanding features are the unique main altar and the ten large stained glass windows depicting the lives of the saints of the Carmelite Order, including St. Therese of Lisieux. Devotions to the Little Flower are held periodically.
(8:00 a.m. to 12:00 p.m. and 3:00 p.m. to 8:00 p.m. M-F; 8:00 a.m. to 9:00 a.m. Sat.; 8:30 a.m. to 6:00 p.m. Sun.)

PRAGUE

336. National Shrine of the Infant Jesus of Prague, St. Wenceslaus Church, 4th and Broadway Streets

Devotion to the Little King had its origin in Czechoslovakia more than 300 years ago. Since many of the settlers of the city originally came from that country, it was only natural that the Discalced Carmelite Fathers would erect a national sanctuary to the Infant here. Established in 1949 in St. Wenceslaus Church, the shrine is located at the intersection of Highways 66 and 92. Novena devotions to the

Infant of Prague are held each month from the 17th to the 25th, with pilgrimages on the Sunday which falls between these dates. In addition to those who attend the services, many others participate by mail. Among the special features of the church are the relics of the true cross and of the manger of Bethlehem. On the lawn south of the Shrine is a large crucifix and the Stations of the Cross. The cross and the outdoor monument to the Infant of Prague are lighted at night. *(7:30 a.m. to 9:00 p.m.)*

OREGON

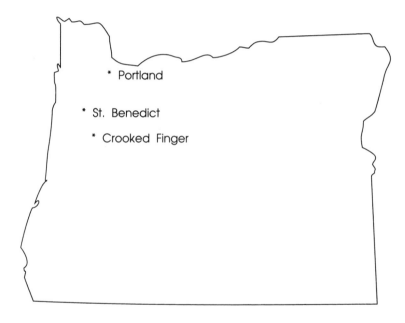

* Portland

* St. Benedict

* Crooked Finger

CROOKED FINGER

337. Holy Rosary Chapel (East of Mount Angel)
Located 12 miles from Mt. Angel in the foothills of the Cascades, the Benedictine church is the scene of an annual Assumption Day pilgrimage. Since 1954, each August 15th brings many old friends — and a few new ones. In the afternoon, there is a procession through the woods while reciting the rosary, then a homily and Benediction. In the early evening there is a rosary procession, then Mass.

Mailing address: c/o St. Mary Church, Mount Angel, Oregon.
(Open during services only)

PORTLAND

338. The Grotto, the National Sanctuary of the Sorrowful Mother, 85th Ave. and Northeast Sandy Blvd.
The world famous shrine is composed of two terraces, one at street level, the other atop a 150-foot cliff. Commanding the entrance to the sanctuary is a crucifixion group in carrara marble. On the lower level is a natural amphitheater facing the cliff. Into its granite walls has been carved a cavern containing a simple white altar and above it, a marble replica of Michelangelo's "Pieta" flanked by two bronze angels. Walking further we find the Fourteen Stations of the Cross, the St. Philip Benizi shrine and the Sunken Gardens. Then there is the Chapel of Mary, Our Mother with its 110-foot bell tower topped by a gold dome and cross. Dominating the interior, above the altar canopy is Jose Desoto's mural depicting the heavenly coronation of Our Lady. A ten-story elevator connects the two terraces. Among the attractions of the upper level is the Sorrowful Mother Grove with its famous wood carving of the Seven Sorrows of Our Lady. And then there is St. Anne's Chapel whose interior walls are lined with a collection of well known Marian paintings and photographic reproductions. The Shrine was founded in 1924 and is served by the Servite Order.
(8:00 a.m. to sunset)

ST. BENEDICT

339. Mt. Angel Abbey (East of Mount Angel)

Founded in 1882 by Fr. Adelhelm Odermatt and a group of Benedictines from Engelberg, Switzerland, the Abbey has been a center of devotion to St. Joseph since its earliest days. Each time Mt. Angel was threatened with financial disaster, fire or building problems, the monks made a novena to the stepfather of Jesus. Help came so soon (and often from unforeseen sources) that it seemed miraculous. Each evening the entire community recites the Litany of St. Joseph. The lower church dedicated to him has a unique baked clay statue of the head of the Holy Family designed by Frances Rich. Each year in March, the monks hold a public novena to St. Joseph in which the local residents and the readers of the Mt. Angel Letter are urged to participate.

(9:00 a.m. to 9:00 p.m.)

TENNESSEE

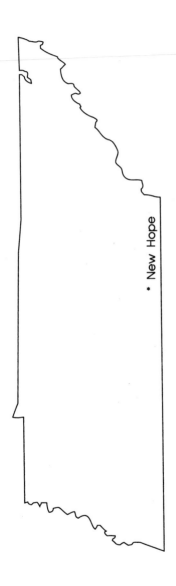

* New Hope

NEW HOPE

340. Virgin of the Poor Shrine

The Benedictine sanctuary is a replica of the shrine at Banneux, Belgium. It was there that the Blessed Virgin, calling herself the Virgin of the Poor, appeared to Mariette Beco in 1933. Located on the property of the Marian Mission, four miles from South Pittsburgh, the shrine was built by Fr. Basil Mattingly O.S.B. in 1976. Soon after the wooden structure's completion, however, it was destroyed by an arsonist. Rebuilt in concrete and stone, the shrine was blessed by Bishop Niedergeses of Nashville six years later. There are devotions (rosary, sermon and litany) each Sunday during May and October. Masses are celebrated at the shrine Saturday mornings May through October.

Mailing address: c/o Our Lady of Lourdes Church, South Pittsburgh, TN

TEXAS

DALLAS

341. Cathedral — Santuario de Guadalupe, 2215 Ross Avenue

Dedicated in 1902, the Sanctuario is the oldest church in the city of Dallas. Formerly known as the Cathedral of the Sacred Heart, the Carmelite church was renamed the Shrine of Our Lady of Guadalupe in 1977. (Of the 5,000 persons attending Sunday Masses at the cathedral, more than ninety percent are of Mexican descent.) Behind the main altar is a needle point tapestry of Our Lady of Guadalupe designed and executed by Fr. B. G. Eades. Measuring 6-feet by 17-feet, it is an enlarged replica of the miraculous tilma of Juan Diego enshrined at Guadalupe, Mexico.
(9:00 a.m. to 5:00 p.m. M-F; 7:30 a.m. to 2:00 p.m. Sun.)

EL PASO

342. Our Lady of Light Church, 4700 Delta Drive

Devotion to *Nuestra Madre Santisima de la Luz* came to this country from Mexico. The Cathedral of Leon holds the original miraculous image brought there in 1732. Painted in accordance to a vision seen by Fr. John Genovsi, SJ, its design is unusual. The Blessed Mother is shown holding the Child Jesus in her right arm, while with her left rescuing a soul about to be swallowed by a dragon symbolizing the devil. The Holy Infant is shown accepting hearts from a basket presented by a kneeling angel. Devotion to Our Lady of Light has been part of this parish's history from its beginning in "Stormville" after the flood of 1897. The church was moved to its present location in 1929 and rebuilt thirty-five years later. Novenas are still held to the Mexican Madonna every Wednesday.
(Open during services only)

343. Mount Cristo Rey

At the summit of a mountain, 4,576 feet above sea level, stands a 42-foot statue of Christ on the Cross designed and built by Urbici Soler, the world famous sculptor. Overlooking two nations and three states, the monument was the inspiration of Fr. Lourdes F. Costa, pastor of San Juan de Cristo Rey Church. Among those present at the 1940 dedication were the Apostolic Delegate to the United States, the Bishop of Sonora, Mexico and Bishop Fulton Sheen, who delivered the English language homily. There is an annual procession up the four-mile road which winds its way to the summit. (The journey takes two hours.)

HOUSTON

344. Our Lady of St. John Church, 7500 Hirsh Road

Devotions to the Blessed Virgin under this title had its origin at the beginning of the 17th century in the Mexican town of San Juan de Los Lagos. It is said that when a child trapeze actor from a traveling circus was killed accidentally during a performance in San Juan, one of the local women rushed to the church to obtain the statue of the Virgin. When it was placed on the little girl's body, the child began to breath again and the wounds healed instantly, leaving no scars.

Devotion to *Nuestra Senora de San Juan* was brought to Houston by Mexican immigrants. The church of Our Lady of St. John has a replica of the original statue and there are frequent novenas and an annual celebration in honor of the Mexican Madonna. In 1987, the famous Marian image from Jalisco, Mexico visited the church for the first time. A number of miracles were reported on that occasion. *(8:30 a.m. to 4:00 p.m. M-F; 7:00 a.m. to 1:00 p.m. Sun.)*

LAMAR

345. Mission of the Confidencia Shrine

Built in 1958, this replica of the Shrine of Our Mother Thrice Admirable in Schoenstatt, Germany is one of more than eighty throughout the world. Located on the Gulf Coast, the Marian sanctuary is also the site of the Schoenstatt Sisters' Provincial Motherhouse and Retreat Center. A pilgrimage to the shrine takes place on the 18th day of each month.

Mailing address: Schoenstatt Sister of Mary, Rockport, TX *(6:00 a.m. to 9:00 p.m.)*

PORT ARTHUR

346. Queen of Peace Shrine, 900-9th Avenue

This popular place of prayer and Marian devotion was built in

1987 by the parishioners of Queen of Vietnam Church. Located across the street from the church, the Queen of Peace Shrine covers one quarter of a block.

SAN ANTONIO

347. St Anthony of Padua Church, 102 Lorenz Road

This Texas city grew up around Mission San Antonio de Valero. The Alamo as it is better known was abandoned late in the 18th century and has never been restored to Catholic worship. It was Fr. Peter Baque's dream to replace the old Mission with a new shrine to St. Anthony. Though the founder of the Missionary Servants of St. Anthony did not live to see it, the church was completed in 1957. There are devotions to the Franciscan saint every Tuesday morning and evening; a Solemn Novena is held from June 5th to 13th. *(8:00 a.m. to 7:00 p.m.)*

348. Shrine of Our Lady of Czestochowa, 138 Beethoven Street

Built by Fr. Peter T. Koltan to honor the Black Madonna of Jasna Gora, the shrine was opened in Poland's Millennial Year, 1966. The Stations of the Cross at the Peace Grotto were made by Walter Marek in the Polish Highland style and blessed by Archbishop Patrick F. Flores. There is a museum attached to the shrine. *(9:00 a.m. to 5:00 p.m.)*

349. National Shrine of the Little Flower, Our Lady of Mt. Carmel and St. Therese, 906 Kentucky Avenue

Inspired by a visit with Mother Agnes and Sister Celine, the two surviving blood-sisters of St. Therese of Lisieux, Fr. Raymond Gomez began construction of this sanctuary to the Saint of the Little Way in 1927. Dedicated four years later, the Discalced Carmelite shrine's architecture shows a combination of Romanesque and Mission styles. The church is flanked by two towers, the larger of which is 160-foot in height and has a carillon of six bells; its companion is surmounted by a 1,000-pound bronze statue of the Little Flower. Rising above the center of the church is a majestic 32-foot dome. The main altar is a masterpiece in marble. Dominating it is "the Gloria" which depicts the cross of Christ beneath which

Our Lady of Mt. Carmel is seen with the Child Jesus on her lap. St. Therese is shown receiving from them roses which she will shower on her clients as graces. The Tomb Chapel, a replica of that at Lisieux, France, has a sepulchre containing a life-sized, hand carved image of the body of the Little Flower.
(Open during services only)

350. Lourdes Shrine of the Southwest, Oblate Drive
To honor their patroness, the Oblates of Mary Immaculate constructed this grotto, said to be the most perfect replica in America of the site of Our Lady's eighteen apparitions at Lourdes, France. The Texas grotto, dedicated on December 7, 1941, Pearl Harbor Day is situated on Oblate Drive on San Antonio's near northside. At the shrine, the statue of the Blessed Mother looks down at the kneeling St. Bernadette. Each day the Oblate Fathers celebrates Masses in the Eucharist Chapel. Throughout the year, twelve novenas are scheduled.

Mailing address: Blanco Road, San Antonio, TX

351. Nuestra Senora de San Juan de los Lagos Church, 3231 El Paso Street
Among the most popular devotions with Hispanics, especially those from Jalisco, Mexico, are those to the *Virgin de San Juan.* Weekly novenas to Our Lady of St. John are held at this Oblate staffed church. Her feast day is February 2nd.
(6:00 a.m. to 8:00 p.m.)

SAN ELIZARIO

352. San Elizario Church
The 14th century French nobleman after whom both the town and church are named, was wedded to Blessed Delphina of Glandieva in 1301. Together they ruled Ansouis and Ariano. Loved by their subjects, they were regarded as an ideal married couple and were known for their piety. St. Elizario was canonized in 1369. A statue of the saint stands above the main altar of this mission church built in 1773. Each September his feast day is celebrated with a Mass and a outdoor procession. The people of San Elizario are also dedicated to

the patron saint of farmers. May 15, St. Isidore's Day is an occasion of great festivity.
(8:00 a.m. to 7:00 p.m.)

SAN JUAN

353. *Virgen de San Juan de Valle Shrine*
Mexicans migrating to Texas from Jalisco, Mexico brought with them devotion to Our Lady of St. John. In 1949, Oblate Fr. Jose Maria Azpianu placed a replica of the famous statue in his parish Church of St. John the Baptist. Soon pilgrims began coming. Fr. Azpianu decided to build a shrine to the Jalisco Madonna. When the Virgen de San Juan de Valle Shrine was dedicated in 1954, 60,000 pilgrims were in attendance. The following years saw rapid expansion: a hotel, a retreat house, a nursing home and a grade school were built. But in 1970 the Marian sanctuary was destroyed when a plane crashed into the church. Though the statue was recovered intact from the flaming wreckage, it took ten years to build a new shrine. In the meanwhile, pilgrims venerated her in a temporary sanctuary set up in the parish cafeteria. Finally, in 1980, the new shrine was dedicated. Among those present were the Apostolic Delegate, Cardinal Humberto Medeiro of Boston and the bishop of Brownsville. The church has a seating capacity of 1,800.
(6:00 a.m. to 9:00 p.m. Sept.-April; 6:30 a.m. to 8:30 p.m. May-Aug.)

SARAGOSA

354. *Our Lady of Guadalupe Shrine*
Rebuilt in 1988 after being completely destroyed by a tornado, the church has been designated as the diocesan shrine to our Lady of Guadalupe by the bishop of El Paso.

Mailing address: c/o Christ the King Church, Balmorea, TX
(9:00 a.m. to 5:00 p.m.)

SOCORRO

355. *La Purisma de Socorro Mission, Socorro Road*
An old legend says that many years ago, when a statue of St. Michael intended for another mission reached Socorro, the hard-carved wooden image became so heavy it could be moved no further. Regarded by the inhabitants of the mission as miraculous,

the *Santo* from Spain still standing in its niche in the sanctuary is the object of much veneration. Founded in 1683 by Indian refugees from the Pueblo Revolt in New Mexico, the Mission of the Most Pure Virgin was swept away by a flood in 1829. The present church, dedicated eleven years later has many of the original *vigas*, decorated hand-carved ceiling beams made in Mexico.

Mailing address: 328 South Nevarez, El Paso, TX *(8:00 a.m. to 6:00 p.m.)*

VIRGINIA

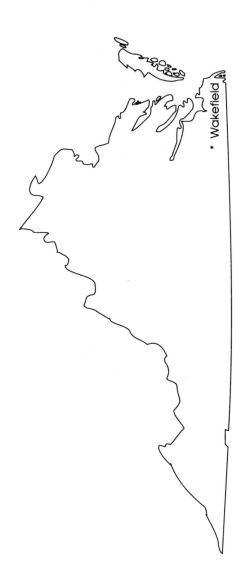

* Wakefield

WAKEFIELD

356. Shrine of the Infant Jesus of Prague, Highway 460

Devotion to the Divine Child under this particular title began in Bohemia during the 17th century and has since spread throughout the world. Located on a busy highway, the Shrine of the Infant Jesus of Prague was dedicated on October 28, 1954. Among its treasures are a replica of the original Czech statue dressed in rich robes and a relic of the True Cross. The shrine is open to the public seven days a week from 6:30 a.m. to 5:30 p.m.

WASHINGTON, D.C.

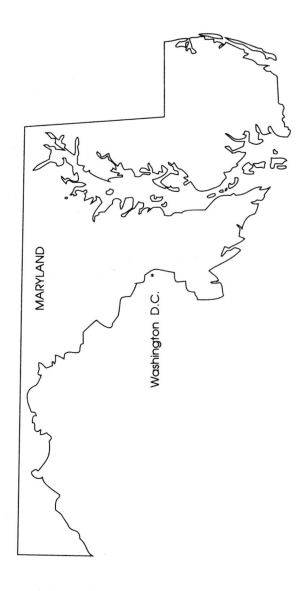

MARYLAND

Washington D.C.

WASHINGTON

357. Ukrainian Catholic National Shrine of Holy Family, 4250 Harewood Road, N.E.

Served by the Redemptorist Fathers, the shrine is located on a 3-acre site a few blocks from the National Shrine of the Immaculate Conception. Though Holy Family Parish was founded in 1949, construction of the Ukrainian sanctuary did not begin until 30-years later. In 1979, during his visit to the United States, Pope John Paul II blessed the cornerstone. Dedicated nine years later, during the Millennium of Christianity in the Ukraine, the Byzantine Rite shrine is still under construction. Designed in a contemporary three-dome Ukrainian style, it will have a seating capacity of 500. An icon of the Holy Family will adorn the sanctuary of the church; above the entrance, a large mosaic will depict the Baptism of the Ukraine. Also, a free-standing bell-tower and a grotto honoring our Lady of Pochayiv will be built.
(Open during services only)

358. Franciscan Monastery, Mount St. Sepulchre, 1400 Quincy Street, N.E.

Since the 13th century, the shrines of the Holy Land have been in the custody of the Order of St. Francis. Dedicated in 1899, the Washington monastery was established by Fr. Godfrey Schilling to popularize their work by exhibiting replicas of famous Roman and Mideastern sanctuaries. The grounds are divided into two parts: the area enclosed within the Rosary Portico and the portion to the south of it. This last includes the Lourdes Grotto, the St. Anne Chapel, the Stations of the Cross, the Grotto of Gethsemane, the Chapel of the Ascension and the Tomb of the Blessed Virgin Mary. The section within the Portico consists of the replica of St. Francis' beloved Portiuncula, the monastery gardens and the church. While the architectural style of the Memorial Church of the Holy Land is modified Byzantine, the floor plan follows the lines of the Five-Fold Cross. The larger central cross is the main body of the church and the four small surrounding ones are represented by the corner chapels to St. Joseph, St. Anthony of Padua, St. Francis of Assisi and St. Mary. At the exact center beneath the central dome is the main altar above which rises the graceful canopy or baldachin supported by four bronze pillars. Also located on the main floor of the church are the Chapel of Penance, a replica of Our Lord's Tomb (the Holy Sepuchre) and the Chapel of the Holy Ghost. Not to be overlooked are the Altar of Calvary, with its crucifixion panel, the Chapel of the Sacred Heart and the Sanctuary of Mt. Tabor memorializing Our Savior's Transfiguration. The lower floor contains the Catacombs with its Martyr's Crypt and the tombs of Sts. Cecilia and Sebastian. Also on this level are the Purgatorial Chapel dedicated to the Faithful Departed and the Grotto of the Annunciation. Finally, there is the Bethlehem Grotto with its Altar of the Magi. Exiting the church on the main floor, the pilgrim will glimpse statues honoring St. Christopher, St. Francis and Fr. Schilling before leaving the monastery grounds.

(9:00 a.m. to 5:00 p.m.)

359. National Shrine of the Immaculate Conception, Michigan Avenue and Fourth Street, N.E.

In 1846, eight years before the promulgation of the dogma of the Immaculate Conception, the bishops of the United States chose the Blessed Virgin, under the title of the Immaculate Conception, as our country's patroness. But it was sixty-eight years before the first step was made toward the creation of a national shrine in her honor. Then in 1914, Bishop Thomas Shahan, rector of the Catholic University of America, received permission from Pope Pius X to build such a Marian sanctuary. Twelve years later, the Crypt Church was completed. But after 1932 lack of funds prevented further construction; there matters stood until the U.S. bishops pledged to raise the needed money during the Marian Year, twenty-two years later. The National Shrine was finally completed and dedicated in 1959. The contemporary Byzantine-Romanesque structure is the largest Catholic Church in America and one of the most immense houses of worship in the world. Built in the form of a Latin Cross, the shrine's most prominent exterior features are the Great Dome (108 feet in diameter); the main entrance with its lofty Roman arch and Rose windows and the Knights Tower, built at the cost of one million dollars. Entering the church, all eyes are drawn to the

3,610-square-foot mosaic of Christ in Majesty at the far end of the sanctuary. Before it stands the impressive marble main altar over which rises a domed baldachin surmounted by a sculpture of Mary Immaculate. The three surrounding apses contain fifteen altars dedicated to the mysteries of the rosary. To the left of the chancel is the Blessed Sacrament Chapel; to the right is the sacristy flanked by mosaics depicting Murillo's "Immaculate Conception" and Titan's "Assumption." Lining the walls of the crossing and the nave are chapels dedicated to St. Mary under ten of her many titles. These are Perpetual Help, Queen of All Hearts, Our Lady of Siluva, Sorrowful Mother, Mt. Carmel, Guadalupe, Czestochowa, Help of Christians, Fatima and Our Lady of the Rosary. Also honored are St. Louise de Merillac, St. Catherine of Siena, St. Vincent de Paul, the Little Flower and St. Dominic. The focal point of the Crypt Church is the Mary Altar, gift of the Marys of America. Standing on a base of Roman Travestine marble, the mensa is a 5,000 pound block of semitransparent golden onyx from Algiers. Surrounding the sanctuary are three apses, each containing five chapels. Those memorialized in the east and west arms are ten holy women, virgins and martyrs of the early church, while the north apse honors the Good Shepherd. That arm has chapels honoring St. Elizabeth, St. Joseph, St. John, St. Anne and the Blessed Sacrament. In 1930-32 the crypt area was expanded southward to include a Lourdes Chapel, a lobby, Memorial Hall and chapels radiating from Memorial Hall, including those honoring Bishop Shahan and St. Pius X. Here the Blessed Virgin is honored by chapels dedicated to her as Queen of the Missions, Our Lady of Bistrica (Croatia), Mother of Good Counsel, the Immaculate Heart, Our Lady of Brezje (Slovenia) and Queen of Peace. In addition there is the Ruthenian-Byzantine Rite Chapel, the Confession Chapel and the Mother Cabrini Memorial. Also, on display is the Tiera of Pope Paul IV which he wore at his coronation.

(7:00 a.m. to 6:00 p.m. M-S; 7:00 a.m. to 7:00 p.m. Sun.)

WEST VIRGINIA

• Boomer

BOOMER

360. St. Anthony's Shrine

Situated on U.S. Route 60, the church dedicated to the patron saint of miners was built in 1928 to meet the needs of an expanding Catholic population. Still a mission church of Immaculate Conception Parish in Montgomery, the shrine is now housed in a new, larger house of worship built in 1954. On the elevated main altar beneath the statue of St. Anthony, in a niche, is a reliquary containing a first-class relic of the Wonder Worker of Padua. A wayside shrine to St. Anthony was erected in 1961.
(Open during services only)

APPENDIX —
SHRINE PATRONS

(The references below refer to specific shrine listings, not page numbers.)

St. Ann — 12, 13, 67, 68, 130, 136, 140, 162, 164, 176, 180, 274, 290, 297

St. Anthony of Padua — 4, 6, 23, 38, 65, 69, 100, 141, 193, 205, 209, 347, 360

Baraga, Bishop Frederick — 184, 186

St. Bernadette Sourbirous — 46

St. Frances (Mother) Cabrini — 70, 147, 276

Casey, Fr. Solanus — 177

Catala, Fr. Magin — 271

Drexel, Bl. Katharine — 99

Dudzik, (Mother) Mary Therese — 157

St. Dymphna — 219

D'Youville, Bl. Marguerite — 134

St. Elzear — 352

St. Francis of Assisi — 15, 141, 224, 230, 231

St. Francis Xavier — 253

Gallitzin, Prince Demetrius — 111, 114

St. George — 246

St. Gerard Majella — 36

Holy Espousals of the Blessed Virgin Mary and Joseph — 21

Holy Family — 357

Holy Relics — 128, 217

St. Isadore — 352

Jesus Christ:
    Agony Grotto — 320
    Blessed Sacrament — 7, 158, 201, 211, 315
    Christ of the Mines — 280
    Christ the King — 251

St. Mary of Mt. Carmel — 93
St. Mary of Seven Dolors — 236
Seven Dolors — 171
Sorrowful Mother — 150, 218, 338
Stella Maris — 37
Virgin of the Poor — 340
"White Lady" — 319
St. Maximillian Kolbe — 105, 158
St. Michael — 355
St. Nicholas — 101
North American Martyrs — 45
St. Odilia — 198
Padre Pio — 80
St.Patrick — 317
St. Paulinus of Nola — 48
St. Peregrine — 151, 270
St. Peter Claver — 316
St. Philippine Duchesne — 175, 313
Poor Souls — 139
St. Rita — 52, 126, 154, 254
St.Roch — 142, 300
Seelos, Fr. Francis — 301
Serra, Bl. Junipera — 260
St. Elizabeth Ann (Mother) Seton — 82, 84, 302, 307
Sulprizo, Bl. Nunzio — 127
Tekakwita, Bl. Kateri — 58
St. Therese of Lisieux — 31, 54, 118, 135, 155, 192, 250, 277, 292, 322, 335, 349
Trinity, Blessed — 249
Uganda Martyrs — 71
St. Vincent Ferrer — 85
St. Walburga — 107

BIBLIOGRAPHY

Attwater, Donald A., *A Dictionary of Mary*. (New York, Longmans, Green & Co., 1956)

Catholic Almanac (Huntington, IN; Our Sunday Visitor, 1988)

Catholic Annual Guide (St. Paul, Normandin Publications, Inc., 1985)

Catholic University of America *New Catholic Encyclopedia* (New York, Mc Graw—Hill, 1967)

Domas, Anna Witz, *Mary, USA* (Huntington, IN; Our Sunday Visitor, 1978)

Hardon, John A. S.J., *Modern Catholic Dictionary* (Garden City, NY; Doubleday & Co., Inc., 1980)

Koenig, Harry C., ed., *A History of the Parishes of the Archdiocese of Chicago* (Archdiocese of Chicago, 1980) 2 vol.

Kreppein, Catherine A., *List of Shrines in the United State and Canada* (Printed Privately, 1988)

Lamberty, Sister Manetta S.C.C., *The Woman in Orbit: Mary's Feasts Everyday Everywhere* (Chicago, The Lamberty Co., Inc., 1966)

Official Catholic Directory (Willmette, IL; P.J. Kenedy and Sons, 1989)

"Pilgrimage Shrines of Our Lady in the United States", *Marian Era*, Vol. IV (1963), p. 140—143

Sullivan, Kay, *The Catholic Tourist Guide* (New York, Merideth Press, 1967)

Thornton, Francis B., *Catholic Shrines in the United States and Canada* (New York: Wilfred Funk, Inc. 1954).

Woods, Ralph L. & Henry F., *Pilgrim Places in North America: A Guide to Catholic Shrines* (New York, Longmans, Green & Co., 1939)

INDEX

(The references below refer to specific shrine listings, not page numbers.)

Hogan, Fr. John R. — 191

Holy Cross — 182

Holy Cross Church (Milwaukee, WI) — 239

Holy Cross Church (Santa Cruz, NM) — 327

Holy Cross — Immaculata Church (Cincinnati, OH) — 209

Holy Cross Fathers — 168

Holy Dormition — 92

Holy Espousals of the Blessed Virgin Mary and St. Joseph, Shrine of (Waltham, MA) — 21

Holy Eucharist — 7, 158, 201, 211, 315

Holy Face Monastery (Clifton, NJ) — 29

Holy Family — 227, 357

Holy Family, Sisters of the — 296

Holy Family, Sons of the — 324, 327

Holy Family, Ukrainian Catholic National Shrine of the (Washington, D.C) — 357

Holy Ghost Fathers — 125

Holy Hill, Shrine of Our Lady of (Hubertus, WI) — 235

Holy House of Loreto (Italy) — 22

Holy House, U.S.A. — 42

Holy Name of the Blessed Virgin Mary Church (Donora, PA) — 103

Holy Relics — 128, 138, 217

Holy Relics, Shrine of the (Maria Stein, OH) — 217

Holy Rosary Church (Chicago, IL) — 142

Holy Rosary Church (Crooked Finger, OR) — 337

Holy Sepulchre — 128, 206

Holy Shroud — 29

Holy Souls — 50

Holy Spirit Adoration Sisters (see Sister Servants of the Holy Spirit)

Holy Spirit, Sanctuary of Mary, Our Lady of the (Branchville, NJ) —27

Holy Stairs (Santa Scala) — 188

Holy Transfiguration Monastery (Redwood Valley, CA) — 266

Holy Trinity Church (New Orleans, LA) — 300

Sorrowful Mother, National Shrine of the
(Portland, OR) — 338
Sorrowful Mother, National Shrine of Our
(Chicago, IL) — 150
Sorrowful Mother Shrine (Marywood, OH) — 218
Sorrows and All Consolation Shrine, Our Lady of
(Linwood, NJ) — 33
Sorrows, Our Lady of — 33, 150, 171, 218, 275, 319, 338
Sorrows, Shrine of Our Lady of (Sycamore, CA — 275;
Starkenburgh, MO — 319)
South Pittsburgh, TN — 340
Southwick, Fr. John J. — 68
Spanish Missions — 253, 260, 270, 271, 284
Spitzig, Fr. Edward — 222
Stack, Fr. Gilbert — 228
Stanisia, Sr. Mary — 242
Star of the Sea, St. Mary — 37
Starkenburg, Our Lady of — 319
Stations of the Cross — 173, 183, 197
Stella Maris Chapel (Newark, NJ) — 37
Stigmatines — 21
Stone House — 307
Strauss, Msgr. Anthony — 318
Strecker, Ignatius — 316
Stritch, Bishop Samuel — 207
Sturbridge, MA — 13
Sugar Creek Mission, KS — 175, 313
Sulpicians — 302, 306
Sulprizo, Francesco — 127
Swarezewska, Our Lady of — 189
Sweeney, Fr. John — 272
Sylvestrine Benedictines — 29
Szemeri, Bela — 24
Szoka, Cardinal Edmund — 194
Talpa, Our Lady of the Rosary of — 264
Tarrish, Dominic — 266

Discover more about Catholic history

Relics, by Joan Carroll Cruz, describes in vivid detail, the stories and history surrounding the major and active relics that are revered by the Catholic Church. Discover the history behind The Holy Manger, The Holy Cross, The Crown of Thorns, The Shroud of Our Lady, and many others. Numerous photos included. No. 701, paper, $10.95, 308 pp.

The Catholic Shrines of Europe, by Gerard E. Sherry, takes you on a journey to ten of the most famous shrines of Europe. The history of each location is thoroughly detailed. A beautiful meditation follows each shrine's description. Shrines included are: Walsingham; Canterbury; Glastonbury; Santiago de Compostela; Our Lady of the Pillar; Lourdes; Miraculous Medal Shrine; Our Lady of Fatima; and more. No. 548, paper, $5.95, 119 pp.

Prices and availability subject to change.

Available at bookstores. Credit card holders may order direct from Our Sunday Visitor by calling toll-free **1-800-348-2440**. Or, send payment plus $3 shipping and handling to: Our Sunday Visitor / 200 Noll Plaza / Huntington, IN 46750.

OUR SUNDAY VISITOR BOOKS

A23BBHBP